Anxiety and Depression

STUART A. MONTGOMERY

St Mary's Hospital, London

WRIGHTSON BIOMEDICAL PUBLISHING LTD
Petersfield

Editorial Office:

Wrightson Biomedical Publishing Ltd
Ash Barn House, Winchester Road, Stroud,
Petersfield, Hampshire GU32 3PN, UK
Telephone: 0730 65647

Distributors:

Blackwell Scientific Publications
Osney Mead, Oxford OX2 0EL, UK
Telephone: 0865 240201

Year Book Medical Publishers
200 North LaSalle Street, Chicago,
Illinois 60601, USA
Telephone: 312 726 9733

British Library Cataloguing in Publication Data
Montgomery, S. A. (Stuart A.)
   Anxiety and depression.
   1. Man. Neuroses: Anxiety 2. Man. Depression
   I. Title
   616.85223

   ISBN 1 871816 02 5

Phototypeset by Scribe Design, Gillingham, Kent
Printed in Great Britain by Biddles Ltd, Guildford.

Anxiety and Depression

Contents

Preface

Anxiety and depression are inextricably linked. The traditional separation into many different disorders has been difficult to apply to the majority of those suffering from mixtures of anxiety and depression. Over the last decade a stricter scientific methodology has been developed both in examining the features and incidence of depression and anxiety in epidemiological surveys in the community, and evolving better measures of depression and anxiety and responses to treatment. It has become clear that many of the older classifications and concepts of illness need to be extensively modified to make way for a more rational scheme which is useful to treatment oriented physicians. The most acceptable classification in a clinical setting is one which encompasses the natural history of the disorder and the modification brought about by treatment.

In attempting to come to an understanding of the many different presentations which are gathered together as anxiety and depression I have tended, therefore, to give prominence to the treatment response data from valid studies. It is also important, of course, to take into account the results from epidemiological studies and outcome studies of long-term treatment and to relegate to the background arbitrary concepts unsupported by data.

This book sets out to examine illnesses from a treatment point of view and aims to provide the busy practitioner with an up-to-date summary of the appropriate treatment approaches for particular conditions and mixtures of conditions, based on positive evidence of efficacy. In coming to a synthesis the book inevitably reflects some degree of personal prejudice. Although I have tried to be objective it is difficult in a new and rapidly changing field, and a certain subjectivity will have crept in.

The attempt at all times is to be practical, to guide the physician in the choice of treatments and in the management of particualr groups. Special emphasis is given to the more recently recognised disorders such as obsessive compulsive disorder, which appears to be a serotonin specific illness, and to the two new concepts which have made their way into the International Classification of Diseases (ICD 10), namely recurrent brief depression and mixed anxiety and depression.

The increasing recognition that depression is a recurrent disorder has changed the emphasis from the treatment of the acute episode, towards long-term treatment of the illness. It is clear from the studies that depression is being under-treated and this book emphasises the role of long-term treatment and gives practical advice on management.

STUART MONTGOMERY

1

Depression and Anxiety

Patients who consult their doctors with depressive or anxious symptoms form a large part of the workload of both general practitioners and specialists, but the majority are treated in the primary care setting. It is unfortunate that the presence of depressive illness, which both anxiety symptoms and depressive symptoms are likely to represent, is frequently missed and many sufferers receive inadequate treatment or do not receive any treatment at all. Depression is a serious and life endangering illness, and also a common one, and its recognition and prompt and appropriate treatment are therefore of the utmost concern.

INCIDENCE

General practitioners know from experience that depression and anxiety are both seen very commonly in the normal population. The epidemiological studies show that some 15% of the general population suffer from either depression or anxiety over a period of 1 year which makes the conditions among the most common illnesses seen. Estimates of the prevalence of depression vary depending on the scope of the population studied and the stringency of the diagnostic criteria used to differentiate illness from normal. A review of the early epidemiological studies reported a life-time risk of developing depression as between 8% and 12% for men and between 20% and 26% for women[1].

A large scale Epidemiological Catchment Area study in the USA[2], has used definitions of illness provided by the DSM III diagnostic criteria to assess the rates of different psychiatric illnesses in the community. In this study the overall life-time prevalence for major depressive episodes with or without a manic episode in the history is reported to be 5.6% (with a higher rate in females than males). The prevalence of any anxiety disorder also appears high with a reported rate of 8.9% over 6 months and 14.6% over life-time.[3] If the illnesses were considered together the rate for any anxiety and any affective disorder was 12.8% over a 6 month period and 19.2% over the life-time. The median age of onset for unipolar major depression in this study was 24 years and lower in bipolar disorder at 18 years. In other words depression is an illness that can appear at an early age, earlier than is perhaps generally recognised. Somewhat higher rates are seen in the Swiss study than in the US study with a 1 year prevalence rate for major depression, minor depression and anxiety disorder taken together of 16.4% in this study. This sample drawn from the normal population is being systematically followed up in Switzerland in a long term epidemiological study which has used rather more careful methodology than some in measuring symptoms.[4] Both studies however agree that depression and anxiety are common in the community.

The number of people in the general population discovered in these studies to be suffering from depression and anxiety was surprisingly high. The levels of morbidity were derived, moreover, on the basis of a rather tough syndromal criterion which would exclude cases falling below the level of a defined syndrome. The implications for primary health care services are serious, the more so when it is remembered that at present not all people who have clearly defined conditions consult a general practitioner. In the Zurich epidemiological study the consultation rate was only 20% for anxiety states or agoraphobia. Somewhat higher levels of consultation were reported for major depression and brief recurrent depression which had a consultation rate of about a third (35%).[5] A similar pattern of a relatively low level of consultation appears to hold in the USA. Approximately 38% of people with major depressive disorder in the ECA study had been seen for treatment in a 6 month period and 20% of those with anxiety disorders. In spite of the large proportion of potential patients who do not consult a doctor, reviews of treatment in primary care have shown that a substantial proportion of general practice is concerned with anxiety or depression. Depression appears to be the most common formal psychiatric disorder representing between 8% and 10% of consecutive consultations in general practice.[6] The repercussion of any increase in consultation rate, which is certainly indicated, could therefore be substantial.

DEPRESSION AND ANXIETY—A SINGLE ILLNESS?

Anxiety and depression are regarded by many physicians in primary care as being a single illness since the majority of their patients have what appears to be mixed anxiety depression, and only a small number present with pure anxiety or pure depression. The International Classification of Diseases (ICD 10) now recognises the mixed anxiety depression syndrome whereas the DSM IIIR of the American Psychiatric Association has a different perception, related largely to hospital psychiatric practice, and proposes what sounds like an easy separation into many different anxiety and depressive syndromes. Who is right?

Classifications of illness can be based on the aetiology, the pathological process involved, or on the appearance of symptoms. In psychiatry little is known about how the disorders arise or about the biological mechanisms and it has been customary to base the separation of illnesses largely on symptomatology. Constellations of symptoms are identified which make up syndromes of illness and, in the absence of demonstrable aetiological factors, these syndromes may be externally validated to some extent by other criteria such as genetic factors, course of illness, response to treatment.

The disagreement between the 'lumpers' who argue for a continuum in psychiatric illness and the 'splitters' who argue for many different illnesses has a very long history since the unitary hypothesis was put forward by Mapother in 1926[7] and supported by Lewis in 1934[8] and the literature on the subject has been extensively reviewed.[9] The main protagonists of a separation between depression and anxiety come from the Newcastle group,[10,11] whose original studies were conducted on inpatients, but they have been supported by studies of both inpatients and outpatients on both sides of the Atlantic.[12,13].

The categorical approach has certainly had the effect of increasing the amount of research in the area although it has not added greatly to our knowledge of the underlying basic processes in the affective disorders. If the different categories represent separate illnesses there must be some external validation of the separation. The justification for separating depression and anxiety put forward in the studies of the Newcastle group was that the distinction is manifest not only in symptomatology, but in the course of the illness, and in response to treatment. More recently, evidence has been accumulating from a number of different lines of research that questions the validity of the separation of anxiety and depression into separate disease states. This evidence comes from studies that have examined the occurrence of anxiety and depression, the development of the illnesses, and the stability of the diagnoses, and also from studies that have tested the specificity of treatments for anxiety or depression. The perception of depression and anxiety as separate illnesses disregards the evidence from epidemiological studies that have consistently reported a substantial overlap between the conditions with many patients fulfilling criteria for a diagnosis of depression as easily as for a diagnosis of anxiety. The Zurich study of rates of illness reports that major depression was found to overlap with anxiety disorders in 36% of cases and there was an overlap of 60% between minor depression and anxiety disorders. In the individuals given a diagnosis of anxiety disorder there was an overlap with major or minor depression of 49%. Studies of groups of patients selected as suffering specifically from anxiety disorders also report a substantial overlap of diagnoses and the occurrence of major depression may be seen in two thirds of patients with agoraphobia and panic

Table 1.1.   Overlapping symptoms of anxiety and depression.

Montgomery and Asberg Depression Rating Scale.

Symptoms seen in anxiety	Symptoms seen in depression
	Sadness
Inner tension	Inner tension
	Inability to feel
	Pessimistic thoughts
	Reduced appetite
Reduced sleep	Reduced sleep
	Lassitude
Concentration difficulties	Concentration difficulties
	Suicidal thoughts

Hamilton Depression Rating Scale.

Symptoms seen in anxiety	Symptoms seen in depression
	Depressed mood
	Guilt
	Suicide
Sleep disturbance	Sleep disturbance
	Psychomotor retardation
Psychic anxiety	Psychic anxiety
Somatic anxiety	Somatic anxiety
Agitation	Agitation
Gastrointestinal disturbance	Gastrointestinal disturbance
Somatic	General somatic symptoms
	Reduced libido
Hypochondriasis	Hypochondriasis
	Loss of insight
	Loss of weight

Hamilton Anxiety Scale.

Symptoms seen in anxiety	Symptoms seen in depression
Anxious mood	
Tension	Tension
Fears	
Insomnia	Insomnia
Intellectual	Concentration difficulties
Depressed mood	Depressed mood
Somatic (muscular)	
Somatic (sensory)	Somatic anxiety
Cardiovascular	Cardiovascular symptoms
Respiratory	
Gastrointestinal	Loss of appetite
Genitourinary	Loss of libido
Autonomic	Autonomic symptoms
Anxious signs/behaviour	Agitation

disorder.[14] The separation of panic disorder, which is currently the focus of much debate, is also questioned by the occurrence of panic attacks in patients diagnosed as suffering from major depression.

Sometimes the depression is considered to have arisen because of the anxiety, in other words to be 'secondary depression', and is reported to occur in between a third and a half of anxious patients.[15,16] An overlap of the magnitude seen in studies which approached the problem from quite different perspectives questions the validity of a separation into different illnesses.

Substantial common symptomatology in depression and anxiety is reported even in studies that claim to demonstrate a separation into two illnesses. For example Mountjoy and Roth in 1982[11] identified certain symptoms which they considered made the differentiation. However 14 of the 16 symptoms they reported as differentiating between neurotic depression and anxiety/phobic states are recognised as important symptoms for registering change in severity of depression and are included either in the Hamilton Rating Scale[17] or the Montgomery and Asberg Rating Scale for depression[18] (see Table 1.1). The items were suicidal thoughts, anorexia, weight loss, poor memory, dizzy attacks, loss of interest, loss of energy, reduced libido, reduced emotional response, compulsions, agitation, fear of being alone, initial insomnia, restless sleep, early wakening, poor concentration; and only two, poor memory and fear of being alone, are not included in these two depression rating scales. Mountjoy and Roth's data provide substantial evidence of the overlap between anxiety and depression.

Depression has anxiety embedded within it: anxiety is one of the most frequently occurring symptoms of depression and also among the most sensitive to improvement or deterioration of the depressive syndrome.[18] It is no accident that the most widely used scales for measuring depression depend in part on anxiety items. What sometimes comes as more of a surprise is that if scales designed for measuring anxiety are compared with scales for measuring depression substantial overlap is seen in the nature of the symptoms enquired about in these so-called separate conditions. Almost all the symptoms included in the anxiety scales have been shown to be useful in registering changes in the severity of depression. The communality of symptoms in patients suffering from depression and those labelled as anxiety states is of course insufficient in itself to establish the two kinds of symptoms as representing the same underlying illness. Taken in conjunction with the other lines of evidence however they form part of an increasingly persuasive argument.

A further indication that there may be a common underlying disturbance in depression and anxiety is the stability of the diagnosis of depression and the relative instability of the diagnosis of anxiety.[19] In the population sample followed up in Zurich the diagnosis of pure anxiety state given on one occasion was only repeated in 10% of individuals on follow up. A substantial proportion of the anxiety states had converted to a diagnosis of depression

(24%) or mixed anxiety/depression (14%). The stability of the diagnosis of depression was much firmer, individuals diagnosed as having depression on the first occasion tended to receive the same diagnosis at follow up.[20] This implies that in some cases anxiety is a form of depression or that it is a prodromal feature of a developing depressive disorder.

Evidence from the studies of family history and possible genetic influences have not helped settle the question of whether there is a continuum in the anxiety/depression conditions. Persuasive similarities have been found in the family history of depression and anxiety states in patients differently diagnosed as having a panic disorder or depression or a combination of the two.[21] Some genetic studies have found evidence to support the concept of two diseases[22] while others report evidence of a genetic influence between panic and depression.[23]

Agreement about a distinction between anxiety and depression would probably have been more easily achieved if different treatments could be shown to be specific for anxiety or depression. In recent years it has become clear, however, that antidepressants have a wider spectrum of efficacy than was previously thought and that, as well as being effective in depression, they may be more effective than conventional anxiolytic treatments such as benzodiazepines in treating anxiety states. For the majority of anxiety states (generalised anxiety, panic, agoraphobia, and probably other phobic states) treatment with antidepressants appears to be effective. While response to the same treatment does not necessarily imply the same aetiology in these conditions it does support the view that there may be an underlying disorder which expresses itself variously in these different states.

The separation of the anxiety states from depression has been one of the areas in psychiatry about which there has been least agreement. For research it may be appropriate to adopt a classificatory system with many divisions if the aim is to examine particular aspects of illness. For the management of patients the trend of recent thinking has been to recognise, as the general practitioner has done for many years, that the separation of anxiety and depression may have been unhelpful and to take account of the substantial overlap between the two diagnoses. Regardless of which view of depression and anxiety is adopted, whether they are manifestations of one illness or are separate illnesses, the questions facing the physician are first, how to recognise the patient who is suffering from depression or anxiety, or mixed anxiety and depression, and, secondly, how to decide on treatment.

REFERENCES

1. Boyd J.H. and Weissman M.M. (1981). Epidemiology of affective disorders. *Archives of General Psychiatry*, **38**, 1039–1046.
2. Burke J.D., Regier D.A. and Christie K.A. (1988). Epidemiology of depression:

recent findings from the NIMH epidemiologic catchment area program. In: *Depression, Anxiety and Aggression* (Ed. J.A. Swinkels and W. Blijleven), Medidact, Houten, 23–38.

3. Weissman M.M., Leaf P.J., Tischler G.L., Blazer D.G., Karno M., Livingston Bruce M. and Florio L.P. (1988). Affective disorders in five United States communities. *Psychological Medicine*, **18**, 141–153.

4. Angst J. and Dobler-Mikola A. (1985). The Zurich study. A continuum from depression to anxiety disorders? *European Archives of Psychiatry and Neurological Sciences*, **235**, 179–186.

5. Angst J. and Dobler-Mikola (1985). The Zurich Study. Recurrent and nonrecurrent brief depression. *European Archives of Psychiatry and Neurological Sciences*, **234**, 408–416.

6. Blacker C.V.R. and Clare A.W. (1987). Depressive disorder in primary care. *British Journal of Psychiatry*, **150**, 737–751.

7. Mapother E. (1926). Discussion on manic-depressive psychosis. *British Medical Journal*, 872–886.

8. Lewis A.J. (1934). Melancholia: A clinical survey of depressive states. A historical review. *Journal of Mental Science*, **80**, 1–42.

9. Klerman G.L. (1977). Anxiety and depression In: *Handbook of Studies on Depression. Studies in Classification, Phenomenology and Aetiology of Depression* (Ed. G.D. Burrows), Excerpta Medica, New York.

10. Gurney C., Roth M., Garside R.F., Kerr T.A. and Schapira K. (1972). Studies in the classification of affective disorders. The relationship between anxiety states and depressive illnesses. *British Journal of Psychiatry*, **121**, 162–166.

11. Mountjoy C.Q. and Roth M. (1982). Studies in the relationship between depressive disorders and anxiety states. *Journal of Affective Disorders*, **4**, 149–161.

12. Coryell W., Noyes R. and Clancy J. (1983). Panic disorder and primary unipolar depression. A comparison of background and outcome. *Journal of Affective Disorders*, **5**, 311–317.

13. Prusoff B. and Klerman G.L. (1974). Differentiating depressed from anxious outpatients. Use of discriminant function analysis for separation of neurotic affective states. *Archives of General Psychiatry*, **30**, 302–309.

14. Breier A., Charney D.S. and Heninger G.R. (1984). Major depression in patients with agoraphobia and panic disorder. *Archives of General Psychiatry*, **41**, 1129–1135.

15. Vollrath M., Koch R. and Angst J. (1990). The Zurich study. Panic disorder and sporadic panic: symptoms, diagnosis, prevalence, and overlap with depression. *European Archives of Psychiatry and Neurological Sciences*, **239**, 221–230.

16. Dealy R.S., Ishiki D.M., Avery D.H. Wilson S.G. and Dunner D.L. (1981). Secondary depression in anxiety disorders. *Comprehensive Psychiatry*, **22**, 612–618.

17. Hamilton M. (1960) A rating scale for depression. *Journal of Neurology, Neurosurgery and Psychiatry*, **23**, 55–62.

18. Montgomery S.A. and Asberg M. (1979). A new depression scale designed to be sensitive to change. *British Journal of Psychiatry*, **134**, 382–389.

19. Eaton W.W. and Ritter C. (1988). Distinguishing anxiety and depression with field survey data. *Psychological Medicine*, **18**, 155–166.

20. Angst J., Vollrath M., Merikangas K.R. and Ernst C. (1990). Comorbidity of anxiety and depression in the Zurich cohort study of young adults. In: *Comorbidity in Anxiety and Mood Disorders* (Ed. J.D. Maser and C.R. Coninger), APA Press, Washington.

21. Vanvalkenburg C., Akiskal H.S., Puzantian V. and Rosenthal T. (1984). Anxious depressions. Clinical family history, and naturalistic outcome. *Journal of Affective Disorders*, **6**, 67–82.
22. Crowe R.R., Noyes R., Pauls D.L. and Slymen D. (1983). A family study of panic disorder. *Archives of General Psychiatry*, **40**, 1065–1069.
23. Leckman J.F., Weissman M.M., Merikangas K.R., Pauls D.L. and Prusoff B.A. (1983). Panic disorder and major depression. Increased risk of depression, alcoholism, panic, and phobic disorders in families of depressed probands with panic disorder. *Archives of General Psychiatry*, **40**, 1055–1060.

2

How to Recognise Depression

Depression has been notoriously difficult to diagnose in general practice. Even when the depression is severe half the cases in the doctor's waiting room apparently go unrecognised[1]. The reasons for this are unclear. It is sometimes suggested that the length of time allotted for the average consultation in primary care is insufficient for the ready recognition of psychiatric symptoms and there is clearly some truth in this. Lack of insight on the part of the patient also undoubtedly contributes and the failure of patients to recognise their own depression has been shown in several studies to reduce the chance of the depression being spotted.

Certain attitudes on the part of both doctors and patients also tend to reduce the likelihood of the diagnosis of depression being given. The stigma attached to illnesses of the mind is strong and the prejudice against psychiatric illness in general and depression in particular may be responsible for some of the bias that exists against giving depression as the diagnosis. There is an often unspoken, but regrettably widely held, belief that depression is self-induced and the well-meant but unhelpful advice to the depressed person to pull themselves together is still all too common. In such a climate of opinion it is easy to understand why patients are reluctant to discuss their problems and expect the doctor, to whom they sometimes attribute unrealistic sensitivity of perception, to initiate the conversation.

Many patients with depression would prefer to have a physical illness. Patients who consult their doctor expect to discuss physical symptoms and in some ways expect to have physical symptoms before contact with the doctor is permitted. The physical symptoms are more likely to be discussed and the causes sought in physical rather than psychological illness. Cultural factors also play their part both in the perception of depression by the patient and in the presentation of symptoms. For example in Middle Eastern, Asian, and some African cultures the concept of depression is poorly formulated and there may be no equivalent word. It is however apparent that the disorder

9

exists in these cultures but there is a greater emphasis on the somatic symptoms which are often ascribed to a presumed illness of the heart or gut. Understandably, these cultural influences linger in people who have moved from their native country and can be a real test of the diagnostic skill of the physician.

Some depression may be missed when it occurs in individuals who are known to their physician because of a current physical illness. The attention is already focused on the physical illness and the presence of depression is overlooked. A sudden increase in complaints about a known chronic physical illness may be the patient's way of expressing the presence of depressive symptoms yet this increase often encourages the doctor to think in terms of a worsening of the physical condition; it may not occur to him to consider the possibility of depression. A sudden increase in complaints should act as a warning and as a signal to enquire about the symptoms of depression.

Attitude towards depression can prove to be an obstacle to treatment in some cases even when depressive symptoms are recognised. The widely held belief that depression and depressive symptoms are normal if they occur after some specified stress has the effect of encouraging the doctor in primary care to enquire more about cause and less about the severity of the illness. The notion that understanding the context of the depression is the major part of treating the illness is mischievous. The implication that removal of the apparently precipitating cause will also remove the depression is a considerable deterrent to patients receiving appropriate treatment and there is the risk that serious depressive illness will be minimised rather than recognised and treated. The presence or absence of 'precipitating causes' has almost no influence on the measures of severity of depression or on the indication for treatment.[2]

THE CORE SYMPTOMS OF DEPRESSION

Physicians need to know which of the many symptoms depressed patients may suffer from most closely identify the illness in order that patients are treated appropriately. In recent years a number of measuring instruments for the severity of depression and its change during treatment have been introduced to meet the needs of research into the efficacy of antidepressant treatments. These scales have had the added benefit of providing much needed help for the practitioner in readily identifying depression as well as in assessing its severity. The objective underlying the construction of the recent scales has been to identify those symptoms which are frequently seen and reliably measured, which reflect most accurately the severity of depression and which individually would be most useful in assessing response to treatment.[3] The principal concern therefore was the measurement of severity and change in those who had already received a diagnosis of depression rather than with the diagnostics. It is nonetheless apparent that individuals with the constellation of symptoms identified with such scales are more likely to have depressive illness than those without. There is considerable agreement across different studies about the identity of these core symptoms.

The close agreement on the most important symptoms of depression can be seen in a comparison between two different diagnostic scales, the Feighner criteria[4] and the DSM IIIR[5] criteria. The Montgomery and Asberg Scale (MADRS)[3] approached the problem from the viewpoint of selecting the most relevant symptoms which were sensitive to change and arrived at a very similar constellation of symptoms. The core symptoms of depression are almost self evident (Table 2.1).

Table 2.1. Core symptoms of depression.

Depression scale (MADRS)[3]	Diagnostic scale (Feighner)[4]	Diagnostic scale (DSM IIIR)[5]
Sadness observed or reported	Dysphoric mood	Depressed mood or irritability
Inner tension		
Loss of interest	Loss of interest	Loss of interest or pleasure
Reduced appetite	Poor appetite	Appetite or weight loss (rarely gain)
Reduced sleep	Sleep difficulty	Sleep loss (or rarely increase)
Concentration difficulties		Diminished concentration
	Agitation or retardation	Psychomotor agitation or retardation
Lassitude	Loss of energy	Loss of energy or fatigue
Pessimism	Self reproach or guilt	Worthlessness or guilt
Suicidal thoughts	Recurrent suicidal thoughts or acts	Recurrent suicidal thoughts or of death

Sadness or depressed mood

In depressed patients the commonest symptom is sadness and it is a symptom which is usually recognised quite easily by the alert practitioner. In severe cases it may not even seem necessary to ask about sadness because it is so obvious from the facial expression and posture.

Sadness is easier to measure than depressed mood partly because it is relatively circumscribed and partly because it does not require a judgement about illness. Sadness can be reliably measured by observation of behaviour or by assessment of what the patients say about themselves. The busy practitioner should be alerted by the presence of obvious sadness or unhappiness to enquire further.

Special care may be needed in assessing sadness in the elderly many of whom may not express complaints on this score, seeming more aware of other somatic symptoms. The elderly depressed are not always treated as promptly as they should be because of an unconscious attitude that they are appropriately low in mood in view of the many losses entailed in the later years of life.

Loss of interest or pleasure

The ability to take an interest and get pleasure from things seems to be one of the universal characteristics of healthy people and its loss a sure indicator of ill health. In the doctor's office depressed patients may well not complain in the first instance of loss of interest or pleasure. They are more likely to complain of feeling out of sorts or generally fed up. Questions about their ability to enjoy their usual interests, hobbies or work may be needed.

In milder degrees of depression this symptom may be too subtle to pick up; in moderate and severe cases the symptom is easy to recognise on appropriate questioning.

Loss of energy or fatigue

Loss of energy is a characteristic symptom of depression which is easily missed in primary care because it is often interpreted as a sign of physical illness. This symptom is characterised by the feeling that everything is an effort, that one needs to push oneself to do things, of being tired before one begins. When this symptom is relatively mild individuals may well describe a general tiredness or lassitude, of things being a bit too much of an effort. In a more pronounced form this loss of energy will be found to interfere with normal social functioning and work. This core symptom is thought by many to be particularly sensitive to treatment.

Loss of sleep

Patients in seeking an explanation for how they feel may already have made the connection with disturbed sleep and may seek 'just something to help them sleep'. Beware of accepting the patient's explanation. Minor changes in sleep patterns are a very accurate measure of depression; patients may report difficulty getting to sleep or in other cases broken sleep and waking early in the morning. They may complain of unsatisfying sleep or having not slept at all well. Individuals vary widely in their sleep requirements or habits and often have an unrealistic expectation of sleep. It is not so much the amount of sleep a patient describes as a change in the pattern of sleep over their recent norm which is a good indicator of disturbance.

Depression is a common cause of persistent sleep problems and, if they have been troublesome for more than 2 weeks, or if they are recurrent, must be taken seriously. Patients who have symptoms of anxiety and sleep disturbance are all too frequently given benzodiazepines as hypnotics to deal with the problem. This may not help the underlying condition as anxiety symptoms with sleep disturbance often indicate the presence of depression.

Pessimism, worthlessness and guilt

A generally pessimistic attitude about the future and feelings of worthlessness, of having let oneself or one's family down are easily recognised if the right questions are asked. It is sometimes helpful to phrase neutral questions: 'have you noticed yourself becoming increasingly optimistic or pessimistic?'. Unfortunately the individual may feel a failure for having these feelings and may try to hide them for fear of the guilt entailed in burdening others. This may discourage them from considering that they have an illness or consulting a doctor.

Thoughts of death or suicide

Feelings that life is not particularly worth living or feelings of being tired of life will alert the doctor to ask specifically about suicidal thoughts. Sometimes there is an unwillingness to ask directly about suicidal intent for fear of provoking an action which the patient had not considered. This is, however, a mistake. Suicidal thoughts are found in some 80% of depressed patients and while patients are often initially reluctant to volunteer that they have thought about harming themselves, if asked directly they seem to welcome the chance to discuss these unpleasant thoughts. Depressed patients may be disappointed if they do not have a chance to air this problem: they may unfortunately take it as a further measure of their own failure, or as a sign of lack of interest on the doctor's part.

Loss of appetite

Some patients may be moderately depressed and still continue to eat normally or in some cases may eat more than usual. Loss of appetite with very marked reduction in food intake is generally found mostly in more severe cases of depression. Relying on appetite loss on its own may be misleading especially in the presence of physical illness. Depressed patients will however often express a lack of enjoyment of, or interest in food, even though they continue to eat. In this sense loss of appetite is common.

Anxiety symptoms in depression

Anxiety symptoms, which are among the commonest symptoms of depression and are very sensitive measures of severity, should be regarded as part of depression. Most diagnostic classificatory systems recognise the presence of anxiety symptoms as integral and there is a good case for regarding the measure of anxiety or distress, such as is included in the ICD 10,[8] or the item inner tension in the MADRS as core symptoms of depression. Certainly, if anxiety symptoms accompany other symptoms of depression the illness is very likely to be depression. It can be confusing when patients appear to have more symptoms of anxiety than they have depressive symptoms and the temptation is to bias the diagnosis to anxiety. Depressed patients may however have a higher level of anxiety even than patients with anxiety states. For example it was shown that in a large group of depressed outpatients a higher score was seen on an anxiety scale than in a similar number of anxious outpatients.[6] The presence of anxiety should accelerate the search for other depressive symptoms.

DURATION OF SYMPTOMS

Duration of the core depressive symptoms is the key to diagnosis. All of the internationally accepted diagnostic scales seem to agree that a minimum duration of 2 weeks is required before a diagnosis of major depression can be entertained. The Feighner criteria[4] suggest that the symptoms should be present for a month but the RDC,[7] the DSM III and DSM IIIR,[5] and the ICD 10[8] all include a minimum duration criterion of 2 weeks. If the individual has symptoms of depression which persist for 2 weeks or more they are likely to be suffering from depression which fulfils criteria for major depression and which will be likely to respond to antidepressants.

Care is needed in establishing the pattern of the onset and the persistence of depression and anxiety symptoms. An abrupt onset with remission after a few days or a week is unlikely to be major depression. The persistence of symptoms for 2 weeks or more is the most important criterion which separates major depressive disorder from brief depression, which in a single episode is not disabling, and from recurrent brief depression which is very disabling (see Chapter 10). The differentiation is important since short-lived mood disturbances have generally not been found to respond well to conventional antidepressants.

The symptoms which persist may not always be those thought of as more conventionally depressive and the presence of anxiety symptoms should not lead to an easy diagnosis of anxiety state. Patients may frequently complain of anxiety symptoms rather than depressive ones and the persistence of anxiety symptoms for a month or more is quite likely to reflect the presence of unrecognised depression. In other patients, whose anxiety symptoms have been persistent, a frank depression subsequently develops.[9] Some patients may appear to have anxiety symptoms on their own in a first illness but if the anxiety becomes established depression seems to follow.

HOW MANY CORE SYMPTOMS EQUAL DEPRESSION?

The presence of depressed mood by itself is not sufficient to justify the diagnosis of depression. Depression is a syndrome not a symptom and this syndrome requires the presence of several symptoms. The DSM IIIR diagnostic system requires five symptoms before the criteria for a diagnosis of major depression are met, one of which must be depressed mood (sadness) or irritability. The syndrome of depression defined by five symptoms undoubtedly responds better to effective antidepressants than placebo but these criteria are seen by some to be too stringent and it is suggested that the minimum cut-off for defining depression requires fewer symptoms. The epidemiological data collected by Angst and colleagues in Zurich have yielded some interesting information on this point.[10] The reporting of symptoms of depression was observed in this study to vary between the sexes, with men having the same degree of impairment from depression as women but reporting fewer symptoms. It appeared that three symptoms were sufficient to define the illness in men and to differentiate the ill from the well; and four symptoms were required in women. The study used carefully trained raters who may have detected symptoms which would be missed in a primary care setting and the requirement for three symptoms in men and four in women for a diagnosis of depression may therefore be seen to be conservative. Under the normal time constraints encountered in a busy practice in primary care, patients who are found to have three core symptoms are likely to have the syndrome of depression and to require treatment. Those who have four or more core symptoms definitely need treatment. Table 2.2 summarises the main aims of the doctor in making the diagnosis of depression.

Table 2.2. The aims of the doctor diagnosing depression.

(a) Establish the presence of anxiety/depression complaints
(b) Identify the core symptoms of depression
　　　three equals probably depression
　　　four or more equals treatable depression
(c) Establish duration of more than 2 weeks

IS IT IMPORTANT TO SUBCATEGORISE MAJOR DEPRESSION?

The distinction between various kinds of depression and the disputes as to whether these distinctions are valid or useful have produced a contradictory and confusing literature. The assumptions which have led to these divisions were never really securely based and recent research has further undermined them.

Psychotic/neurotic—An unhelpful distinction

The traditional division of psychiatric illnesses into the broad categories of psychosis and neurosis has the unfortunate effect of imposing a rather wide separation of 'psychotic' depression from 'neurotic' depression. There is an implication in the division into separate categories that separate treatments exist for psychotic and neurotic depression and the further implication that neurotic depression may be related to underlying personality and may not therefore be amenable to treatment.

The division into psychotic and neurotic depression is mirrored by other categorisations using different titles to cover fairly similar concepts. Psychotic depression has been variously referred to as endogenous, vital, melancholic, biological or nuclear depression whereas neurotic depression has been variously termed reactive, anxious or personality disordered depression.

Much of the heat generated in the controversy as to whether depression is one illness hinges around statistical manipulations of the symptom complexes of depression in an endeavour to decide whether there is a separate subgroup of depression characterised by an 'endogenous' pattern of symptoms. Does it matter? From a practical viewpoint it would matter if there were differences in the age of onset, in the course of the illness, or in response to treatment which would affect the management of patients. In fact the age of onset and course of the illness appear to be the same for those with an endogenous pattern as for the rest of depression and the evidence for a differential response to treatment weak. Both groups, for example, show a clear response to treatment with antidepressants compared with placebo.

There has been some evidence that a narrowly defined group of depressions, labelled endogenous, may be more persistent and associated with such 'biological' symptoms as weight loss, early morning wakening, retardation, and diurnal variation. This more homogeneous group has been the focus of much biological research into the possible underlying mechanisms of depression on the grounds that the homogeneity would make it possible to focus on the critical variables. In fact the differences demonstrated between endogenous and nonendogenous or reactive depression are not impressive in the contribution they have made to the management of depressed patients.

Reactive depression

Endogenous depression has in the past been contrasted with reactive depression, perceived by some as neurotic and others as a reaction to environmental stressors which will respond to changes in the environment rather than to treatment. Precipitating life events appear, however, in almost all large studies to be associated to a similar degree with both endogenous and non-endogenous depression and therefore have little value in helping to discriminate between these groups. In other words the term 'reactive' has proved to be misleading. The concept of reactive depression has arguably done much harm by encouraging doctors to concentrate on understanding the social or psychological context rather than to find the most effective treatment.

Treatment response in subcategories of depression

It has been thought that the presence of endogenous features predicts the best response to antidepressant treatment but this seems to be too narrow a view. The best response was found in one study in 1979[11] in patients with mixed features of neurotic and endogenous depression shown in their intermediate scores on the Newcastle diagnostic index (1965)[12] rather than those with very high 'endogeneity' scores. Although early studies reported that the best response to antidepressants was seen in patients categorised as endogenous not all studies have found this advantage compared with neurotic depression.[13] A recent large study also found a poorer response in patients with 'nuclear depression' (endogenous) who were in this case more severely ill.[14] There was an element of circularity in some studies which attempted to identify separate categories of depression. For example in the Newcastle studies one of the identifying features of 'reactive' depression was a previous inadequate response to treatment and it may well be that such self fulfilling definitions have biased the results.

The classification system of the American Psychiatric Association puts depression into a single category. Both the current DSM IIIR and the earlier versions have eliminated the separate categories of neurotic or endogenous depression, placing both together as major depressive disorder. The diagnosis of depression is based on the syndrome of depressive symptoms and on their persistence over a period of at least 2 weeks. The notion of cause in the sense of precipitating events has no part to play. Comprehensive investigation of treatment response has been able to report that this larger depressive group defined in the DSM III responds well to antidepressants independently of the proportion of endogenous patients included and consistently better than placebo in large multicentre studies. This important finding makes it necessary to consider that both endogenous and neurotic depression require treatment with antidepressants.

For the purposes of treatment it would make sense to abandon this division into categories of endogenous or reactive depression and to regard depression as an illness requiring treatment whose presentation varies slightly in different individuals, cultures and settings.

Retarded depression

Retardation, when it is present, has been shown in many analyses to be a good predictor of response to treatment. The problem rests with the identification of this factor of psychomotor retardation on its own which is only seen in about half of the depressed population. The concept is sometimes widened to include poor concentration, loss of energy, loss of interest, loss of sleep and appetite. In this very wide definition retarded depression appears little different from conventional depression. The French concept of 'inhibitory states' reflects the wider concept and it is no surprise that the treatments most in use for these conditions are antidepressants. The concept has some advantages in that it bypasses the stigma of depression and yet allows appropriate treatment. Claims are made that some antidepressants are more effective than others in treating retarded depression but there is no consistent evidence to support the claims.

Agitated depression

In some severe depressions the individual is both agitated and retarded, being both restless and slowed down, so that it is often difficult to separate the factors. Agitation is only rated as a symptom in about a quarter of moderately or severely depressed patients and only a proportion of these would be thought of as suffering from agitated depression. It was, in the past, thought that agitated depression required specific treatment with sedating drugs and it has been a fairly common habit to treat the anxiety symptoms of depression symptomatically with antidepressants which have marked sedative properties. The wisdom of this approach has been brought seriously into question with the development of the new class of antidepressants which are non-sedative. It appears that anxiety within depression may have a better response to treatment with these antidepressants than with sedative tricyclic antidepressants as studies with zimelidine, fluvoxamine, and fluoxetine have shown (see Chapter 7).

DYSTHYMIA

Chronic depression is unfortunately common. A proportion of patients seem to develop a long-term relapsing course of illness compounded by inadequate and inappropriate treatment. Dysthymia, a fairly recent addition to the various categories of affective disorders in DSM III, is proposed as a condition characterised by low grade grumbling depressive symptoms which are present most days for 2 years. To fulfil the DSM IIIR diagnostic criteria for dysthymia, patients must have depressed mood plus two other depressive symptoms. In other words it is very similar to major depression except that the symptomatology is both mild and chronic. The number of patients who fulfil the criterion for dysthymia by having three symptoms of major depression but who have not developed the full illness as defined in DSM IIIR is likely to be very small. A substantial overlap with major depression of some 50% is seen and also of some 30% with patients who have recurrent brief episodes of depression.[15]

The treatment studies in this condition are difficult to interpret because of the potential for overlap with other diagnoses. Some of the patients who fulfil the diagnostic criteria for pure dysthymia may in reality be suffering from major depression that has been attenuated by less than adequate treatment. Others may have been treated without success and may have resistant depression. Patients with recurrent brief depression are also likely to receive a diagnosis of dysthymia as it is sometimes possible to obtain a history of apparent chronic depression in individuals who have in fact been suffering from frequently occurring episodes of brief depression. Our own and our patients' memory for distant events is often unreliable and the diagnosis of dysthymia, which depends on an accurate memory of symptoms over a 2 year period, is often unfortunately suspect.

The studies on dysthymia which have been published show a very high proportion of patients have major depression on top of dysthymia. For example, in a study which demonstrated the efficacy of imipramine in dysthymia, 94% of the patients with dysthymia had concomitant major depression.[16] The value of this diagnostic concept will depend very largely on treatments being shown to be effective in patients who are clearly identified as suffering from dysthymia without concomitant depression. No such studies have yet been published.

SEVERITY OF DEPRESSION

The severity of the illness is an important practical consideration in deciding whether to institute treatment with an antidepressant. The evidence that antidepressants are effective compared with placebo is generally confined to studies which have examined carefully defined groups of depressed patients with sufficient scores on rating scales to be classified as moderate to severe depressive illness. Studies of treatment in mild depression have by and large failed to find clear cut efficacy for antidepressants or for that matter any other treatment.

Clearly in any group categorised as mild depression there will be some patients whose illness is more severe than others and which is more likely to respond to antidepressants. Differentiating between the very mild depressive symptoms for which the efficacy of antidepressants is uncertain and patients with more severe depression that would benefit from antidepressant treatment may not always be easy. There have however been some studies of the efficacy of antidepressants used in the general practice setting that have thrown some light on the lower levels of severity of depression where antidepressants may still be shown to be effective. One study, which used the Hamilton Rating Scale for depression scores to define severity, suggested that the point below which a difference between an antidepressant and placebo is not seen seems to lie somewhere around a score of 13 on the 17 item scale.[17] This compares with a score for recovery which is usually taken as a score of 6 to 8, and for moderate depression, the minimum entry criterion to the usual antidepressant efficacy study, as a score of 16 to 18.

Mild symptoms of depression cannot however be dismissed lightly. Some of the patients with mild symptoms may well be developing moderate depression which definitely requires treatment. Others of those thought to have mild depression have indeed symptoms which are more severe but which are difficult to elicit, particularly in the primary care setting. The depressed patients who are apparently most difficult to identify in primary care are those with concomitant physical symptoms, those with little insight or realisation that they are depressed, and of course men who may be expected to report fewer symptoms. The presence of any of these factors should make one pause before dismissing the illness as mild.

Table 2.3. Summary of factors which may obscure depression in general practice.

1. Precipitating 'cause' does not obviate need for treatment
2. Look for the presence of anything more than minimal symptomatology
3. Do not ignore the depression in order to treat anxiety
4. If clouded by physical symptoms ask about depression in greater detail

REFERENCES

1. Freeling P., Rao B.M., Paykel E.S., Sireling L.I. and Burton R.H. (1985). Unrecognised depression in general practice. *British Medical Journal*, **290**, 1880–1883.
2. Paykel E.S., Rao B.M. and Taylor C.M. (1984). Life stress and symptom pattern in outpatient depression. *Psychological Medicine*, **14**, 559–568.

3. Montgomery S.A. and Asberg M. (1979). A new depression scale designed to be sensitive to change. *British Journal of Psychiatry,* **134**, 382–389.
4. Feighner J.P., Robins E., Guze S.B., Woodruff R.A., Winokur G. and Munz R. (1972). Diagnostic criteria for use in psychiatric research. *Archives of General Psychiatry,* **26**, 57–63.
5. American Psychiatric Association (1987). *Diagnostic and Statistical Manual of Mental Disorders. Third edition Revised.* American Psychiatric Association, Washington.
6. Prusoff B. and Klerman G.L. (1974). Differentiating depressed from anxious neurotic out-patients. *Archives of General Psychiatry,* **30**, 302–309.
7. Spitzer R., Endicott J. and Robins E. (1975). *Research Diagnostic Criteria. Instrument No. 58,* State Psychiatric Institute, New York.
8. WHO (1990). *International Classification of Diseases. Revision 10.* World Health Organisation, Geneva.
9. Noyes R., Clancy J., Hoenk P. and Slymen D.J. (1980). The prognosis of anxiety neurosis. *Archives of General Psychiatry,* **37**, 172–178.
10. Angst J. and Dobler-Mikola A. (1984). The Zurich study. Diagnosis of depression. *European Archives of Psychiatry and Neurological Sciences,* **234**, 30–37.
11. Rao V.A. and Coppen A. (1979). Classification of depression and response to amitriptyline therapy. *Psychological Medicine,* **9**, 321–325.
12. Carney M.W.P., Roth M. and Garside R.F. (1965). The diagnosis of depressive symptoms and the prediction of ECT response. *British Journal of Psychiatry,* **111**, 659–674.
13. Simpson G.M., Lee H.L., Cuche Z. and Kellner R. (1976). Two doses of imipramine in hospitalized endogenous and neurotic depressions. *Archives of General Psychiatry,* **33**, 1093–1102.
14. Grove W.M., Andreasen N.C., Young M., Endicott J., Keller M.B., Hirschfeld R.M.A. and Reich T. (1987). Isolation and characterization of a nuclear depressive syndrome. *Psychological Medicine,* **17**, 471–484.
15. Angst J., Vollrath M. and Koch R. (1988). New aspects on epidemiology of depression. In: *Lofepramine in the Treatment of Depressive Disorders* (Ed. J. Angst and B. Woggon), Vieweg, Braunschweig, 1–14.
16. Kocsis J.H., Frances A.J., Voss C., Mann J J., Mason B.J. and Sweeney J. (1988). Imipramine treatment for chronic depression. *Archives of General Psychiatry,* **45**, 253–257.
17. Rowan P.R., Paykel E.S. and Parker R.R. (1982). Phenelzine and amitriptyline: effects on symptoms of neurotic depression. *British Journal of Psychiatry,* **140**, 475–483.

3

Anxiety

NORMAL ANXIETY

A certain level of anxiety is normal from time to time in everyday life and may often serve the useful function of spurring us on to necessary action. The emotion of anxiety would be experienced as normal if it was appropriate to the circumstances, and accepted as a natural concomitant of the arousal needed to deal with a particular situation. The symptoms, both psychic and somatic, which include feelings of fear and panic, palpitations, sweating, trembling, etc, evoked by a feared circumstance such as perhaps an examination or a public performance are familiar to us all.

In the basic 'fight and flight' paradigm the emotion of anxiety results from the sympathetic autonomic response to the frightening stimulus and also enhances the appropriate response. Performance may well be improved by the emotion and there is certainly no reason to assume that we would necessarily benefit if we never experienced feelings of anxiety. The borderline between what we can accept as normal anxiety and pathological levels is determined largely by the level of functioning of the anxious individual. Where the anxiety is such that appropriate response can no longer be made to the stresses of daily life, work, or relationships, help is needed although this help will not necessarily take the form of medication.

ANXIOUS PATIENTS IN PRIMARY CARE

Patients who are suffering from a variety of complaints loosely grouped under the heading of anxiety disorders make up a large part of the case load of the general practitioner. The proportion of these who are treated with anxiolytic drugs is substantial, inflated both by the ready recognition of anxiety symptoms on the part of the general practitioner and by the apparent unwillingness of patients to tolerate this kind of discomfort. The wide media coverage currently given to the stress of living in the Western world and its negative effects on the human condition might lead us to think that the demand for extensive anxiolytic treatments is a relatively new phenomenon. On the contrary, throughout history we have always sought pharmacological means to relieve our burdens be it with opiates or cocaine, or the use of alcohol or tobacco.

Until recently the majority of the patients treated for anxiety with a pharmacological agent in general practice would be most likely to have received an anxiolytic drug such as a benzodiazepine for symptomatic relief[1,2]. The approach to the diagnosis of anxiety and to its management is however changing with the increasing perception that many of these patients have not been receiving appropriate treatment.

An apparent willingness in the past to burden the normal feelings of anxiety in response to life's stresses with an illness label was probably encouraged by the generally held belief that benzodiazepines were completely harmless drugs that could therefore be freely prescribed for the rapid relief of minor anxiety symptoms. The recognition of the very real risks of dependence with these drugs, if used for more than very short courses, should lead to a reassessment of the wisdom of labelling brief periods of anxiety, which are normal, as though they represented an illness in need of treatment.

This is not to advocate the view that psychological suffering should always be borne stoically without assistance. The doctor's role is to relieve suffering to the benefit of the patient and where there is an illness, intervention may be required. We have, however, come to recognise that much of what was treated medically as anxiety in the recent past probably did not merit pharmacological treatment at all. People whose apparent symptoms of anxiety are in fact a normal reaction to everyday problems, or to more major life events, may not be best served by the prescription of anxiolytic drugs which can cause more difficulties than they solve.

IS IT DEPRESSION?

Many patients who are treated for anxiety states are in fact suffering from other illnesses. Numerous studies have shown for example that psychological illness is frequently missed in general practice and in particular that depression, even if it is severe, may be overlooked[3-5]. Many of the cases given a diagnosis of anxiety state or no diagnosis at all by the primary care physician would be given a diagnosis of depression by a psychiatrist.

Anxiety may be diagnosed more frequently than depression because anxiety is perceived as a more acceptable condition by patients, who will complain readily of somatic symptoms of anxiety but may be slow to describe frank depressive symptoms. The concept of anxiety is in some sense comforting; it provides a diagnosis which is not apparently medical and which has links with everyday language. The description of someone as anxious contains the clear idea that something has made them anxious. The diagnosis permits a discussion about the understandability of the state and of what the patient sees as the cause, whether relevant or not. When we describe our patients as anxious, they presume we mean what they mean: that there is a normal and understandable reaction to life's stresses which results in a natural increase in anxiety. They are reassured by the thought that there is no substantive illness requiring vigorous treatment, rather an understandable state for which a little help is appropriate.

The coexistence of anxiety and depressive symptoms in depressive illness is of course well documented. It would therefore be unwise to use anxiety symptoms on their own to discriminate between anxiety states and depressive illness. As patients are quite likely to report their anxiety symptoms rather than their depressive symptoms the wise physician will want to probe further in case there is underlying depression. A reliable strategy in investigating a patient presenting with anxiety but in whom there are also depressive symptoms is to consider the likelihood that the individual is in fact suffering from depression.

DIAGNOSTIC CATEGORIES IN ANXIETY

Psychiatry has not been particularly helpful to the primary care physician in providing guidelines for the diagnosis and management of anxiety states. The traditional classification of anxiety disorders assumed the existence of separate kinds of anxiety. The assumptions implied a difference from each other both in their presentation and in their differential response to treatment modalities. The conceptualisation of a group of anxiety disorders which are responsive to behavioural treatments and others which are responsive to anxiolytic drugs has however been undermined by the recognition that the different proposed subgroups are not treatment-specific. A further complication has been that a large proportion of what had been traditionally considered as anxiety disorders are seen to fall within a broader concept of depressive illness.

DEFINITIONS OF ANXIETY IN DSM IIIR

The DSM IIIR diagnostic system[6] of the American Psychiatric Association has tended to split anxiety disorders into smaller and smaller subgroups

Table 3.1. Categories of anxiety disorders
according to DSM IIIR.

- Panic disorder with agoraphobia
- Panic disorder without agoraphobia
- Agoraphobia without history of panic disorder
- Social phobia
- Simple phobia
- Obsessive compulsive disorder
- Generalised anxiety disorder

although the justification for this on the basis of differential treatment or
prognosis is not immediately apparent. The resulting number of categories
discussed here may be too large to be particularly useful to an ordinary
practitioner whose business is choosing the best treatment for appropriate
patients (see Table 3.1).

PANIC DISORDER

The pivotal features of panic disorder are unexpected attacks of panic which
are often sudden in onset with intense fear and a range of somatic symptoms
such as palpitations, choking, dizziness, trembling, sweating, etc. The
symptoms are inexplicable and often so distressing that the individual fears
he or she may be dying or going crazy and suicide attempts are not
uncommon, particularly if there is concomitant depression. The panic
subsides usually after an hour but may recur again with little or no
provocation within a few days and often leads to avoiding situations in which
an attack had previously been experienced, where an attack would be
embarrassing, or where help might not easily be available. The avoidance
reaction leads to a constricted lifestyle and in severe cases the sufferer may
become completely housebound.

Panic disorder is a relatively recent concept and was only introduced into
the DSM III system in 1980. The view on panic seems to have developed
since it was first described as a separate diagnostic entity and in the current
revision of the DSM system panic disorders have been given a rather more
inclusive definition. Originally a diagnostic criterion of three attacks in 3
weeks had to be fulfilled for a diagnosis of panic disorder. It is hard to specify
the exact number of attacks that defines the illness. The earlier criterion has
been modified in DSM IIIR to include those who have a persistent fear of
an attack for a month following a panic attack. Panic disorder now subsumes
much of the area formerly labelled agoraphobia on the grounds that the
withdrawal manifested by patients suffering from panic as a defence against

the possibility of a panic attack should not be considered a separate illness. This broadening of the definition leads to a considerable overlap with other anxiety disorders.

Patients who can be categorised as suffering from panic disorder readily present for treatment in primary care. It can be a disabling illness and decreased work quality was reported by 83% of panic patients in one survey, while 67% said they had either lost their job or taken a reduction in income, and 50% complained of their inability to drive. From recent epidemiological studies it appears that patients with panic disorder tend to seek treatment more readily when, as is frequently the case, they are also suffering from depression.[7]

The recognition of panic disorder has not been accepted with the same enthusiasm in Europe as is apparent in the USA. For example the recent consensus meeting in the UK[8] did not recognise panic as a separate disorder and its status as a diagnostic entity is still regarded by some as controversial. The concept has some descriptive validity although the definitions in the DSM IIIR are questioned to some extent by the finding that patients may have periods with less frequent attacks, and by epidemiological research which finds a substantial number of individuals in the community who suffer from severe panic attacks but at a lower frequency.[9,10] Some patients may also confuse panic attacks with anxiety about a panic attack and they may therefore overestimate the number of attacks. Some support for the diagnostic separation of panic disorders is provided by the increased prevalence in the families of patients with panic disorder and the suggestion of a possible genetic link[11] but the co-occurrence of depression makes it difficult to interpret these data. The overlap of panic disorder with depression is substantial: 50–75% of panic patients suffering from depression at some stage and 15–30% of patients with major depression suffering from panic during the index episode.[12,13] This overlap remains the largest obstacle to the acceptance of panic disorder as a separate disorder. Those who suffer from both panic disorder and major depression are seen to have a higher suicide attempt rate: 23% compared with pure panic where it is only 7% in the ECA study in the USA and this suggests that the combined diagnosis should be viewed more seriously.

AGORAPHOBIA

This is defined as the unreasonable fear of being in situations from which escape may be difficult or embarrassing or in which help may not be available. As a result of this fear situations may be avoided such as travelling by bus, or tube, or being in a crowd or going out of the home alone. Agoraphobia may be closely allied to social phobias, e.g. examination nerves, fear of public speaking. The situation always provokes intense anxiety with many physical symptoms.

PHOBIA

Phobias are thought of as the persistent fear, recognised as unreasonable, of a particular animal or defined situation which provokes an immediate and predictable anxiety response accompanied by somatic anxiety symptoms such as palpitations, choking, sweating, panicky feelings. Common examples are fear of snakes, spiders, mice, cats, heights, lifts, enclosed spaces which lead to avoiding these situations, the thought of which is often sufficient to strike fear into the heart of the phobic person. These phobias are subdivided into simple, involving a single fear, or multiple. Those affecting social performance are subgrouped as social phobias.

OBSESSIVE COMPULSIVE DISORDER

Obsessive compulsive disorder (OCD) is characterised by recurrent obsessions or compulsions which are distressing, time consuming, and interfere with normal functioning at work or socially. There is very often phobic avoidance of situations which relate to the content of the obsessions, e.g. a person with an obsession about dirt might avoid public conveniences. The single difference between phobias as currently defined in DSM III and the obsessions of OCD is that phobias should have a persistent fear of a circumscribed stimulus or situation and in OCD the fear need not be circumscribed and must persist for more than an hour a day. Obsessive compulsive disorder is discussed separately (see Chapter 9) in view of the emerging evidence that this is a separate illness with pharmacological specificity.

GENERALISED ANXIETY

Generalised anxiety is characterised by excessive worrying over trifles, which persists for 6 months or more, accompanied by symptoms of anxiety such as tension, autonomic arousal, irritability, and concentration difficulties. In the revised DSM III categorisation patients with these symptoms who do not fulfil the criteria of panic disorder, agoraphobia, etc., are given the separate label of generalised anxiety disorder. The status of this group is problematic since the DSM III suggests that incapacity in this condition is rarely of greater than mild severity. The duration of the anxiety symptoms is probably the pivotal criterion for generalised anxiety disorder and is thought by many to be too narrow using the 6 month criterion.

OVERLAP OF SUBGROUPS OF ANXIETY

In practice the dividing lines between most of these diagnostic subgroupings, which appear clear in the formal classifications, are much less satisfyingly distinct in patients. Panic is currently considered by many to be a distinct syndrome and is a good example of the problem. The distinction drawn between panic with and without agoraphobia, and agoraphobia without panic may be a useful directive for carefully examining the phenomena but the practical validity of the proposed distinction is less obvious. As most practitioners know, panic disorder or agoraphobia frequently arise in individuals with a history of general anxiety or phobic anxiety, and disentangling the interrelationships between these conditions is no easy task. It seems possible that the nosological differentiation may be reflecting differences in severity or differences in presentation of the same underlying illness.

The overlap between panic and depression is a further complication that has to be taken into account in assessing anxious patients. The symptom of panic, which is integral to the measurement of the item inner tension in the Montgomery and Asberg Depression rating scale,[14] is a sensitive measure of the severity of depression. The panic symptoms within depression do not appear to be independent of the depression and by and large improve both with spontaneous remission of the depression and in response to antidepressant treatment. Depression which develops 'secondary' to the panic may occur in as many as 50–75% of patients.

WHAT SHOULD WE DO?

The separation of anxiety into numerous subcategories is of interest in research but does not have immediate practical value for the practitioner in primary care where most anxious patients are treated. The primary care physician would do well to concentrate first on the likelihood of depression being present in the patient who consults with symptoms of anxiety and to give priority to its treatment. Once the possibility of depression has been eliminated the most useful separation of anxiety is to recognise those patients with mild anxiety or those with simple phobias which are likely to respond to reassurance, anxiety management advice or behavioural treatments and to differentiate them from those with the more severe conditions which are more likely to need pharmacological treatment.

Table 3.2 shows four questions the physician should be able to answer before attempting to treat an anxious patient.

Table 3.2.   Management of anxious
patients.

1. Is it normal anxiety?
2. Is it depression?
3. Is it mild anxiety, or simple phobia?
4. Is it moderate or more severe anxiety?

REFERENCES

1. Clare A.W. and Williams P. (1981). Factors leading to psychotropic drug treatment. In: *The Misuse of Psychotropic Drugs.* Gaskell Books, London.
2. Skegg D.G.G., Doll R. and Perry J. (1977). Use of medicines in general practice. *British Medical Journal,* **1,** 1561–1563.
3. Goldberg D. and Blackwell B. (1970). Psychiatric illness in general practice. *British Medical Journal,* **2,** 429–443.
4. Weissman M.M. and Klerman G.L. (1977). The chronic depressive in the community: unrecognized and poorly treated. *Comprehensive Psychiatry,* **18,** 523–532.
5. Freeling P., Rao B.M., Paykel E.S. Sireling L.I. and Burton R.H. (1985). Unrecognised depression in general practice. *British Medical Journal,* **290,** 1880–1883.
6. American Psychiatric Association (1987). *Diagnostic and Statistical Manual of Mental Disorders, Third edition, Revised.* American Psychiatric Association, Washington.
7. Vollrath M. and Angst J. (1990). Outcome of panic and depression in a seven year follow-up: results of the Zurich Study. *Acta Psychiatrica Scandinavica,* in press.
8. Ashcroft G.W., Beaumont G., Bonn J., Brandon S., Briggs A., Clark D., Davison K., Gelder M.G., Goldberg D., Herrington R., Khan M.C., Lader M., Lipsedge M.S., MacDonald A., McGuire P., Millan P.T.S., McInnay K.M., Stinton R.F., Sims A.C.P., Snaith R.P. and Wheatley D. (1987). Consensus statement on panic disorder. *British Journal of Psychiatry,* **150,** 557–558.
9. Katon W. (1986). Panic disorder: epidemiology, diagnosis, and treatment in primary care. *Journal of Clinical Psychiatry,* **47,** 21–27.
10. von Korff M.R., Eaton W.W. and Keyl P.M. (1985). The epidemiology of panic attacks and panic disorder. *American Journal of Epidemiology,* **122,** 970–981.
11. Torgerson S. (1983). Genetic factors in anxiety disorders. *Archives of General Psychiatry,* **40,** 1085–1089
12. Mountjoy C.Q. and Roth M. (1982). Studies in the relationship between depressive disorders and anxiety states. *Journal of Affective Disorders,* **4,** 127–147.
13. Leckman J.F., Weissman M.M., Merikangas K.R., Pauls D.L. and Prvsoff B.A. (1983). Panic disorder in major depression. *Archives of General Psychiatry,* **40,** 1055–1060.
14. Montgomery S.A. and Asberg M. (1979). A new depression scale designed to be sensitive to change. *British Journal of Psychiatry,* **134,** 382–389.

4

Which Antidepressant? A Review of the Older Treatments

OLDER TRICYCLIC ANTIDEPRESSANTS

The older tricyclic antidepressants include amitriptyline, nortriptyline, clomipramine, imipramine, protriptyline and trimipramine. These are discussed in the following sections.

The efficacy of TCAs

When antidepressants were first introduced some 30 years ago they represented a major advance in the treatment of depression. They brought about far reaching improvements in the quality of life of depressed patients and enabled most patients to be adequately treated in the community. They are now used so widely and taken so much for granted that we tend to forget how relatively recently they were developed.

The efficacy of the first antidepressants, the tricyclics, was established initially in uncontrolled clinical practice but over the years they have been quite thoroughly evaluated in comparative placebo-controlled studies. There is now a substantial body of knowledge on their efficacy because some are used as reference comparators in the efficacy testing of new potential antidepressants. The strength of the evidence of their effectiveness is impressive and, although there are some studies which failed to record a difference from placebo, their efficacy cannot be seriously challenged.

The tricyclic antidepressants (TCAs) have a broad spectrum of efficacy and exert a beneficial effect across the various subcategories of depression. Some studies have suggested that patients with more biological symptoms of depression who might be categorised as 'endogenous' respond best to TCAs although others suggest they do less well.[1,2] The numerous studies demonstrating an effect in patients with 'neurotic' or 'reactive' depression suggest this view is too limited and that TCAs are effective across the range of depressed patients. There is however a caveat as it appears that patients who score very highly on a scale of endogenous features such as the Newcastle Diagnostic Index or those who have delusions may respond less well to TCAs and better to ECT.[3,4]. Although the progress heralded by the early TCAs should not be ignored, they have obvious shortcomings, such as the delay in onset of action and the lack of response in 30–40% of patients. Though there may be some alleviation of symptoms when any treatment is initiated, comparisons with placebo reveal a delay of some 2 weeks or more before response to an antidepressant, rather than to non-pharmacological variables begins to appear, and not all patients respond. It has been something of a disappointment to clinicians that, in spite of more than a generation of development, even the newer antidepressants do not have a better response rate than the TCAs and they do not appear to work any more quickly.

Since there is little to choose between the antidepressants available in terms of efficacy the choice will be based primarily on safety and the likely side effects. In this respect there is much to criticise in the performance of the older TCAs. They were used widely when they were introduced because they represented an important improvement in treatment. Their continued wide use in spite of their shortcomings even though there are newer safer drugs available has to be attributed to some extent to the inertia of familiarity.

Differences between TCAs

The level of response does not seem to differ between the various TCAs so that one compound does not particularly recommend itself above the others. There is also no clear basis for selecting a particular TCA for an individual patient in order to improve the chance of response. The TCAs have a range of mixed pharmacological actions with effects on noradrenergic, serotonergic, cholinergic, histaminic, and muscarinic receptors and any differences in their profile of efficacy are relatively minor.

Some TCAs are characterised by having a very substantial sedative effect and others somewhat less, due to differential effects on the histamine receptors, and this has led to a categorisation into sedative and 'alerting' TCAs (Table 4.1). Some clinicians have asserted that these properties can be used to achieve an improved response in particular types of depressed patients. The notion of a sedative antidepressant producing a better response in depressed patients with anxious symptoms, and an alerting antidepressant for those with features of retardation is attractive but, with clear evidence to the contrary, misleading. All effective antidepressants appear to have the same efficacy in improving retardation and the sedative tricyclics appear if

Table 4.1. Differences in sedative effects of the older TCAs.

Marked sedative effect	Less sedative effect
Amitryptiline	Imipramine
Dothipein	Nortriptyline
Doxepin	Desipramine
Clomipramine	Protriptyline

anything to be less effective in treating the anxiety associated with depression than non-sedative antidepressants[5-7].

It may be more important for some patients than others to avoid sedative effects, for example if a patient is trying to continue at work, and this will affect the choice of prescription. However, the appearance of side effects depends to some extent on the individual and some patients will complain about the sedative effects of an antidepressant which others are able to tolerate.

The only TCA that appears to have a selective effect is clomipramine which was observed, soon after its development, to have a differential effect in alleviating obsessive compulsive symptoms in depression. It has since come to be used preferentially in depression where these symptoms are prominent and also in obsessive compulsive disorder where it has been shown to be effective both in the presence and absence of depression (see Chapter 9).

Side effects of older TCAs

There is much more concern now about the safety of prescribed medication than was the case when the TCAs were first introduced and we now expect antidepressants to have a proven record of safety. Many potential antidepressants are rejected very early in development because of unwanted side effects. The higher standards of safety now imposed would probably have the effect of eliminating many of the commonly used older TCAs if they were discovered now.

Familiarity with the TCAs is a major reason for their continued wide usage and because of familiarity the importance of their side effects tends to be underestimated. Clinicians are conditioned to expect the unpleasant anticholinergic and sedative effects associated with the older TCAs (Table 4.2). Indeed dosage is often titrated against the appearance of side effects although the rationale for this practice has been criticised.

The anticholinergic side effects which can be very troublesome represent a major disadvantage of the older TCAs. Patients are often unable to tolerate them and their consequent failure to comply with taking medication

Table 4.2.   Side effects occurring frequently with tricyclic antidepressants.

Anticholinergic	Cardiovascular	Other
Dry mouth	Postural hypotension	Sedation
Blurred vision	Tachycardia	Nausea
Constipation	Dysrhythmias	Impotence
Hesitancy of micturition		Weight gain
Tremor		

compromises treatment. Although in many cases the side effects are better tolerated after the first 2 weeks of treatment, a substantial proportion of patients will continue to be troubled for longer than this. In any case, if, as is often the case, the side effects are very marked patients will not be prepared to persevere even for 2 weeks. The therapeutic effect may be delayed for this long and if the patient experiences only the unpleasant side effects, with no apparent compensatory alleviation of the depression, it is not surprising if they give up the treatment.

Cardiovascular effects of older TCAs

It has to be remembered that effects that are tolerated by some patients can have serious consequences in others. The TCAs are associated with cardiovascular effects which can be dangerous, particularly in overdose. Minor ST changes on the ECG following exercise were reported as long ago as 1961 in depressed patients being treated with imipramine.[8] Since then there have been numerous reports of cardiac abnormalities during treatment with TCAs in therapeutic doses as well as in overdosage. Some clinicians have suggested that the dangers of cardiotoxicity with the TCAs have been given undue prominence and that the risk need not be considered in patients with intact cardiac function. However, this overlooks the fact that a substantial proportion of depressed patients are elderly and are therefore more at risk of undetected cardiac disease. Moreover, postural hypotension is common, and while it may not cause more than inconvenience in younger patients, it is a risk in the elderly with the possibility of fractures resulting from falls.[9,10] It is safer to avoid the risk of these cardiovascular effects by avoiding TCAs in the elderly and this limits the usefulness of these antidepressants.

It is also an unfortunate fact that medication given to treat depressed patients is sometimes used by those patients to harm themselves. The cardiotoxic effects of the TCAs, which are increased with higher dosages and with high plasma drug concentrations,[11] contribute to the poor record of safety in overdose of the TCAs. Arrhythmias and decreased contractility of the myocardium are reported to be important causes of death following overdose with TCAs.[12] The cardiotoxic effects of the older TCAs cannot therefore be disregarded.

Serious adverse drug reactions

Most of the medicines in use, if they are effective in treatment, are also associated with some risk. With antidepressants these risks include cardiotoxicity, liver reactions, convulsions, blood dyscrasias, hypersensitivity and immuno-allergic reactions. The familiarity of the older drugs can bring about a false sense of security and there is a tendency for physicians to drop their guard and to overlook adverse reactions or, if they do recognise them, not to report them. Certain adverse drug reactions (ADR) are so well known with older drugs that clinicians may feel that it is no longer necessary to report them. A similar bias applies to published reports where editors would be interested in publishing new findings with new drugs but not in repeat findings with old drugs. As a result the true incidence of such side effects is undoubtedly higher with the older drugs than the official statistics suggest.

One way of reducing the bias of differential reporting of adverse reactions with new compared with old drugs is provided by the comparisons of a new compound with a reference TCA and placebo made during the development programme of a putative antidepressant. During these clinical trials all side effects, and especially serious ADRs, are monitored very closely and are usually reported by the investigator without knowledge of which compound, be it new drug, reference antidepressant or placebo, is associated with the side effect.

Estimates of the incidence of convulsions associated with TCAs, for example, appear substantially lower when open reporting systems are considered than when the data from clinical trials are examined. The incidence of convulsions during treatment with imipramine reported in the clinical trials was 1–2%.[13] The reports of convulsions associated with maprotiline during early clinical trials were at a similar level of 0.46–1.6% (28 in 1750 patients)[14] although in later studies in the United States, possibly using lower dosages, the incidence with maprotiline was 0.41%. There have been similar reports of an unacceptably high incidence of convulsions of 0.5–1% associated with higher doses of dothiepin and of clomipramine. These figures compare badly with the lower rate seen in clinical trials with the newer antidepressants such as viloxazine, fluvoxamine and fluoxetine.

Imipramine

The first of the antidepressants was discovered by chance in the perceptive open study of Kuhn in 1956 and is now used widely as a reference antidepressant in placebo-controlled studies. Although imipramine has less sedative properties than amitriptyline it is nevertheless more sedative than some of the neutral non-sedative antidepressants. Characterised inappropriately as alerting and therefore, according to one theory, useful in retarded depressives it has been shown to be effective across the range of depression and also to be more effective than chlordiazepoxide in anxiety disorders.[15] In common with other TCAs there is a delay in onset of effect and a lack of efficacy in around a third of patients. Imipramine is used in lower doses in the UK than in the United States and there is some disagreement about the minimum effective dose. The higher doses used in the USA have been shown to produce an unacceptable level of convulsions and other unwanted effects. In common with the other older TCAs imipramine has significant cardiovascular effects and is associated with deaths in overdosage.[16] Serious ADRs including hepatotoxicity, and blood dyscrasias are also reported. It has the advantage of being relatively inexpensive but this does not seem sufficient justification for its prescription since safer alternatives exist. The marked anticholinergic effects, dry mouth, blurred vision, tremor are often cited as reasons for poor compliance and failure of treatment.

Amitriptyline

Amitriptyline is still the most widely used antidepressant in the world in spite of its danger in overdose which is now widely recognised (see Chapter 12). It is undoubtedly effective as an antidepressant in major depression as the large placebo-controlled trials over the last decade have shown. It is associated with cardiotoxic effects and serious ADRs such as convulsions, dyscrasias, and hepatotoxicity, at levels which would cause concern in a recently marketed antidepressant. Amitriptyline is one of the most sedative TCAs as well as having some of the most marked anticholinergic effects. It is contraindicated in patients with cardiac problems, and also in patients with urinary hesitancy, or incipient glaucoma. Because of the danger of amitriptyline in overdose its prescription should be avoided in patients with a history of suicidal attempt or indeed with marked suicidal thoughts.

Clomipramine

Of the older TCAs clomipramine is the one with the most evidence of selectivity of antidepressant action. There is good evidence of efficacy compared with placebo although there is a high incidence of unacceptable side effects, such as convulsions, and drug interreactions. It is also associated with provoking sexual difficulties such as difficulty in achieving orgasm. It is the antidepressant most commonly associated with sudden death following its use in combination with monoamine oxidase inhibitors. Despite its toxicity, clomipramine appears to be relatively safe in overdosage. Clomipramine has a reputation of being more effective in severe depression although this has not been systematically investigated. It is used preferentially in treating obsessive compulsive disorder both with and without concomitant depression.

NEWER TRICYCLIC ANTIDEPRESSANTS

The newer tricyclic antidepressants include dothiepin, doxepin, maprotiline and lofepramine. With the exception of lofepramine these newcomers to the group of TCAs differ little from the traditional antidepressants in their clinical effects. This was to be expected from their similar basic chemical structure and pharmacological actions. They are apparently as effective as the older compounds in the same range of patients. There is little to choose between the older TCAs in their lack of tolerability and efforts to produce newer TCAs with fewer and less severe side effects have not always met with success.

Dothiepin

It has been suggested that dothiepin, which is a very sedative drug, is better tolerated than the earlier TCAs. However, it may have acquired this reputation because it is frequently used in very low doses. The disadvantage of this is that efficacy has not been adequately demonstrated at these low doses[17] and if dothiepin is prescribed in the high doses where efficacy can be demonstrated against placebo, the incidence of serious side effects, such as convulsions, is unacceptably high[18]. The analysis of deaths attributable to overdose with individual TCAs shows that of the TCAs in common use, dothiepin and amitriptyline, which are associated with some 50 deaths per million patients treated,[16] are the most dangerous in overdose. In an illness like depression, which carries a substantial risk of a suicide attempt which is difficult to predict, these drugs should only be used with great caution, or avoided in favour of safer alternatives.

Maprotiline

Slight differences in chemical structure led to maprotiline being somewhat misleadingly described as a tetracyclic compound and labelled as a second generation antidepressant to differentiate it from the TCAs. However the chemical difference is small and the profile of maprotiline's pharmacological effects carries the same disadvantages as the traditional TCAs. In particular, maprotiline appears to be more likely than some antidepressants to induce seizures at therapeutic doses even in non-epileptic patients and this disadvantage is seen even more clearly in overdose. A recent study showed that despite the clear-cut efficacy in long-term treatment of depression with maprotiline[19] there was a significant and worrying increase in suicide attempts in the patients treated with maprotiline compared with placebo. This points to a dissociation between the provocation of suicide attempts and the effective treatment of depression.

Doxepin

When doxepin was originally introduced it was thought to be less cardiotoxic than amitriptyline. The early studies that supported this opinion appear to have been inadequate and doxepin has been shown to be one of the antidepressants most commonly associated with deaths in overdose in the elderly.[20] In the light of the real reduction in cardiotoxicity seen with newer antidepressants, introduced more recently, the use of doxepin on grounds of safety is questionable. When deaths from overdose with antidepressants are taken into account, doxepin appears to be far from safe.

Lofepramine

The only TCA with significant improved safety in overdose compared with the older TCAs is lofepramine. This antidepressant, which appears to be as effective as the older TCAs, has a much improved profile of side effects and lacks important anticholinergic and cardiotoxic effects. It is well tolerated by patients and is therefore likely to be a useful antidepressant for patients who have a low tolerance of side effects. As well as being well tolerated in therapeutic dosage it appears to be much safer in overdosage than the older TCAs. On the first 1.5 million prescriptions of lofepramine there were no reported deaths from overdose with lofepramine alone.[21] There have been a number of reports recently of abnormal liver function tests with lofepramine which appear to be reversible.[22] Some reports would be expected since the incidence of transient liver function changes with reference TCAs in double blind trials is in the region of 1%. There is no evidence to date to suggest the rate is higher with lofepramine.

WHICH TCA TO USE

The older TCAs represented progress when they were first introduced and clinicians were right to use them widely. Safer drugs that are better tolerated have, however, been developed since then and these should be the first choice of prescription. There may be a tendency to opt for one of the older TCAs because it is familiar and more recently, in the current climate of financial constraints on treatment, because they are cheap. It is important, however, to take account of the disadvantages of the TCAs in assessing the true cost of treatment.

Of the 'new' tricyclic antidepressants the only one with advantages in terms of safety is lofepramine which appears to be one of the safest antidepressants in overdose. A question however still remains about its hepatotoxicity. Death from overdosage is by far the most serious risk in treating patients in their own home and of the TCAs lofepramine is therefore the most suitable.

MONOAMINE OXIDASE INHIBITORS

The monoamine oxidase inhibitors (MAOIs) include tranylcypromine, phenelzine and isocarboxazid. They were introduced before the days of stringent efficacy testing and there is much uncertainty about their therapeutic role, how effective they really are, and in what kind of patients. Although the MAOIs were reported to be more effective than placebo, quite early in their history substantial studies found that they were less effective than the TCAs in major depression and as more effective antidepressants became available the MAOIs have tended to be displaced.[23,24] Subsequent studies in a broader range of depressed patients have not been much more encouraging.[25]

Some clinicians found the MAOIs to be effective in certain kinds of patients and claims are made that they are of particular benefit for patients with so-called atypical depressions associated with anxious, hysterical, or somatic features, with increased sleep or appetite.[26] The evidence for a selective effect is however not strong though there are suggestions that efficacy is greater in the presence of concomitant anxiety.[25,27]

Attempts at delineating patients who might respond differentially to MAOIs continue to be made, however, and two recent reports from the USA provide some support for the notion that MAOIs may be effective for anxious or 'atypically' depressed patients.[28,29] Phenelzine was found to be better than imipramine in these studies which selected patients who were defined as having minor depression with a proportion suffering from the symptoms used to describe atypical depression, such as rejection sensitivity and hysteroid dysphoria. Atypical depression is a concept rather than a clearly defined and widely accepted diagnostic group, and a closer look at the kind of patients included in these studies suggests that about half may have been suffering from episodes of brief depression. The indication that MAOIs may be helpful in these patients, who are difficult to treat with conventional antidepressants, needs replication.

The MAOIs are not as effective as other available treatments in major depression and further controlled studies would be needed before a recommendation for their use in specific subgroups of patients could be justified. They also have other well known disadvantages which makes the choice of another antidepressant preferable.

Patients may complain of anticholinergic side effects with the MAOIs although these may be less severe than with the older TCAs. It is their additional, potentially dangerous side effects which lead clinicians to prefer to prescribe a conventional, safer antidepressant. Dietary amines can be absorbed without being metabolised in the gut and liver and this can cause hypertension and even hypertensive crises. Patients have therefore to be warned to avoid foods which are rich in amines. Some of the foods often included on the forbidden list, such as pickled herrings and snails, may not be too much of a problem to avoid but others such as cheese, beer, yeast and yeast products, and chocolate are common. In the UK it is now thought by some that the risks from unwise dietary intake have been exaggerated but in some other European countries, for example France, hypertensive crises with MAOIs are considered to be a substantial risk. With the possible exception of moclobemide, a new MAOI thought to be associated with lower tyramine interreactions, MAOIs should only be used in patients who are able to comply with dietary restrictions.

A more dangerous problem than the dietary restrictions demanded with the MAOIs is their potentiation of the effects of directly or indirectly acting sympathomimetic drugs including over the counter cough mixtures, and the adverse reactions that can arise by their concomitant use with a range of other commonly used drugs. The co-prescription of contraindicated drugs can be avoided by the practitioner and patients can be warned to avoid over the counter proprietary medicines. It is however often forgotten that these restrictions should be continued after the end of therapy while the drug is still being eliminated. Starting therapy with other medication at this point can have unwanted consequences. Serious adverse reactions, including rapid death from hyperthermia, have been reported with a combination of MAOIs and clomipramine or the new 5-HT uptake inhibitors, and extra caution is needed in view of the fact that a large series of 5-HT uptake inhibitors is now reaching the market.[30-32] MAOIs should not be used in combination with any 5-HT uptake inhibitor because of the risk of provoking the sometimes rapidly fatal neuroleptic malignant syndrome.

Moclobemide

There has been progress in the development of new MAOIs with the synthesis of inhibitors of the separate MAOA and MAOB enzymes. The MAOB inhibitors, which would not be expected to produce the tyramine response since MAOB is selective for dopamine, have not yet proved useful as antidepressants. The doses at which antidepressant effects might be seen appear to be sufficiently high for any specificity to be lost. Effort has therefore been concentrated on producing reversible short-acting MAOA inhibitors which do not require the synthesis of new MAO enzyme to restore function. This could lead to MAOI antidepressants which are free of the 'cheese' effect, which limits the older MAOIs. Moclobemide, now reaching the market, has short-acting MAOA inhibition although inhibition of MAOB is also seen, possibly because of active metabolites. It seems from the clinical testing programme that antidepressant efficacy may be seen at a dose which is low enough to avoid the 'cheese' effect and if this is borne out in wide usage it may turn out to be a useful drug.[33,34]

ECT

The use of ECT is confined in many parts of the world for the most part to the treatment of last resort, where other treatments have failed, where a patient is known from the history to respond poorly to antidepressant drugs, or where the depressive illness is immediately life endangering. ECT is nevertheless our oldest and possibly most effective treatment. As might be expected, most of the assessments of efficacy have been carried out in hospital inpatients who were suffering from severe depression and all but one of the studies which compared ECT with simulated ECT found positive treatment effects. The same category of severely ill patients has been examined in comparisons between ECT and antidepressants although not with double blind controls. For the most part ECT is found to be superior to antidepressants and no studies have found that antidepressants are superior.[35,36]

It is of course possible that in a wider range of patients the superiority of ECT could be less marked. Some of the studies which endeavoured to identify the characteristics which predicted a good response to ECT found that those with depressive delusions respond best and it is suggested that patients with 'neurotic' features respond least well.[37]

ECT is likely to remain the treatment reserved for severe depression which is not responsive to antidepressants or in which the risk of delay in response of conventional antidepressants cannot be borne.

REFERENCES

1. Morris J.B. and Beck A.T. (1974). The efficacy of antidepressant drugs. *Archives of General Psychiatry*, **30**, 667–674.
2. Rogers S.C. and Clay P.M. (1975). A statistical review of controlled trials of imipramine and placebo in the treatment of depressive illness. *British Journal of Psychiatry*, **127**, 599–603.

3. Rao V.A. and Coppen A. (1979). Classification of depression and response to amitriptyline therapy. *Psychological Medicine*, **9**, 321–325.
4. Glassman A.H., Kanter S.J. and Shostak M. (1975). Depression, delusions and drug response. *American Journal of Psychiatry*, **132**, 716–719.
5. Montgomery S. A., McAuley R., Rani S.J., Roy D. and Montgomery D.B. (1981). A double blind comparison of zimelidine and amitriptyline in endogenous depression. *Acta Psychiatrica Scandinavica*, **63** (Suppl. 290), 314–327.
6. Montgomery S.A. (1989). The efficacy of fluoxetine as an antidepressant in the short and long term. *International Clinical Psychopharmacology*, **4** (S1), 113–119.
7. Wakelin J. (1988). The role of serotonin in depression and suicide. *Advances in Biological Psychiatry*, **17**, 70–83.
8. Kristiansen E.S. (1961). Cardiac complications during treatment with imipramine (Tofranil). *Acta Psychiatrica Neurologica*, **36**, 427–442.
9. Glassman A.H. and Bigger J.T. (1981). Cardiovascular effects of therapeutic doses of tricyclic antidepressants. A review. *Archives of General Psychiatry*, **38**, 815–820.
10. Orme M.L'E. (1984). Antidepressants and heart disease. *British Medical Journal*, **289**, 1–2.
11. Spiker D.G., Weiss A.N., Chang S.S., Ruwitch J.F. and Biggs J.T. (1975). Tricyclic antidepressant overdose: clinical presentation and plasma levels. *Clinical Pharmacology and Therapeutics*, **18**, 539–546.
12. Frommer D.A., Kulig K.W., Marx J.A. and Rumack B. (1987). Tricyclic antidepressant overdose. *Journal of the American Medical Association*, **257**, 521–526.
13. Geltzer, J. (1986). Limits to chemotherapy of depression. *Psychopathology*, **19**, 108–117.
14. Dillier N. (1982). Worldwide clinical experience with Ludiomil. *Activitas Nervosa Superior (Praha)*, **24**, 40–52.
15. Kahn R.J., McNair D.M., Lipman R.S., Covi L., Rickels K., Downing R., Fisher S. and Frankenthaler L.M. (1986). Imipramine and chlordiazepoxide in depressive and anxiety disorders II Efficacy in anxious out-patients. *Archives of General Psychiatry*, **43**, 79–85.
16. Montgomery S.A. and Pinder R.M. (1987). Do some antidepressants promote suicide? *Psychopharmacology*, **92**, 265–266.
17. Thompson C. and Thompson C.M. (1989). The prescribing of antidepressants in general practice II: A placebo trial of low-dose dothiepin. *Human Psychopharmacology*, **4**, 191–204.
18. Montgomery S.A., Baldwin D. and Green M. (1989). Why do amitriptyline and dothiepin appear to be so dangerous in overdose? *Acta Psychiatrica Scandinavica*, **80** (Suppl. 354), 47–54.
19. Rouillon F., Phillips R., Serrurier D., Ansart E. and Gerard M.J. (1989). Rechutes de depression unipolaire et efficacite de la maprotiline. *L'Encephale*, **15**, 527–34.
20. Farmer R.D.T. and Pinder R.M. (1989). Why do fatal overdose rates vary? *Acta Psychiatrica Scandinavica*, **80** (Suppl. 354), 25–36.
21. Cassidy S. and Henry J. (1987). Fatal toxicity of antidepressant drugs in overdose. *British Medical Journal*, **295**, 1021–1024.
22. Committee on Safety of Medicines (1988). Lofepramine (Gamanil) and abnormal tests of liver function. *Current Problems*, **23**.
23. Medical Research Council (1965). Clinical trial of the treatment of depressive illness. *British Medical Journal*, **1**, 881–886.

24. Young J.P.R., Lader M.H. and Huges W.C. (1979). Controlled trial of trimipramine, monoamine oxidase inhibitors, and combined treatment in depressed out-patients. *British Medical Journal*, **2**, 1315-1317.
25. Paykel E.G., Rowan P.R., Parker R.R. and Bhat A.V. (1982). Response to phenelzine and amitriptyline in subtypes of outpatient depression. *Archives of General Psychiatry*, **39**, 1041-1049.
26. Quitkin F.M., Rifkin A., and Klein D.F. (1979). Monamine oxidase inhibitors: a review of antidepressant effectiveness. *Archives of General Psychiatry*, **36**, 749-760.
27. Sheehan D.V., Ballenger J.C. and Jacobsen G. (1980). Treatment of endogenous anxiety with phobic, hysterical, and hypochondriacal symptoms. *Archives of General Psychiatry*, **37**, 51-59.
28. Liebowitz M.R., Quitkin F.M., Stewart J.W., McGrath P.J., Harrison W.M., Markowitz J.S., Rabkin J.G., Tricamo E., Goetz D.M. and Klein D.F. (1988). Antidepressant specificity in atypical depression. *Archives of General Psychiatry*, **45**, 129-137.
29. Quitkin F.M., Stewart J.W., McGrath P.J., Liebowitz M.R., Harrison W.M., Tricamo E., Klein D.F., Rabkin J.G., Markowitz J.S. and Wagner S.G (1988). Phenelzine versus imipramine in the treatment of probable atypical depression: defining syndrome boundaries of selective MAOI responders. *American Journal of Psychiatry*, **145**, 306-318.
30. Committee on Safety of Medicines (1985). Adverse reactions to antidepressants. *British Medical Journal*, **291**, 1638.
31. Committee on Safety of Medicines (1988). Fluvoxamine (Faverin): adverse reaction profile. *Current Problems*, **22**.
32. Committee on Safety of Medicines (1989). Fluvoxamine and fluoxetine—interaction with monoamine oxidase inhibitors, lithium and tryptophan. *Current Problems*, **26**.
33. Larsen J.K., Holm P. and Mikkelsen P.L. (1984). Moclobemide and clomipramine in the treatment of depression. *Acta Psychiatrica Scandinavica*, **70**, 254-260.
34. Versiani M., Oggero U., Alterwain P., Capponi R., Dajas F., Heinze-Martin G., Marquez C.A., Poleo M.A., Rivero-Almanzor L.E., Rossel L., Schmid-Burgk W. and Ucha Udabe R. (1989). A double-blind comparative trial of moclobemide vs. imipramine and placebo in major depressive episodes. *British Journal of Psychiatry*, **155**, Suppl. 6, 72-77.
35. Pippard J. and Ellem L. (1981). *Electroconvulsive Therapy in Great Britain 1980*. Gaskell, London.
36. Fink M. (1987). ECT: a last resort treatment for resistant depression? In: *Treating Resistant Depression* (Ed. J. Zohar and R.H. Belmaker). PMA Publishing, New York, pp. 163-174.
37. Crow T.J., Deakin J.F.W., Johnstone E.C., MacMillan J.J., Owens D.G.C., Lawler P., Frith C.D., Stevens M. and McPherson K. (1984). The Northwick Park ECT trial: predictors of response to real and simulated ECT. *British Journal of Psychiatry*, **144**, 227-237.

5

Newer Antidepressant Treatments

General dissatisfaction with the older tricyclic antidepressants (TCAs) and the recognition that better antidepressants were needed which would be more effective, safer, and have fewer side effects led to the introduction of a number of new antidepressant drugs.

ADVANTAGES OF NEWER ANTIDEPRESSANTS

The hope of improved efficacy in a wider spectrum of depressed patients has not been fulfilled with the new antidepressants: they appear to be as effective as the older TCAs but no more so and are no quicker to exert an antidepressant effect. Optimistic reporting usually attributes early onset of action to any new antidepressant but it soon becomes clear that there is the customary delay of 2 weeks or more before an extra response over placebo is seen. In some patients there is of course some response earlier than this but, as with all antidepressants, a significant difference from placebo is not reliably seen before a month has passed in the conventional studies. In very large studies or a metanalysis of large data sets significant efficacy may be seen earlier.

The advantage of the newer antidepressants is that they have fewer side effects than the TCAs and are in general therefore better tolerated by patients. The importance of this cannot be overemphasised since treatment with the older TCAs is often compromised by lack of compliance by patients who are unwilling to suffer the often extremely unpleasant effects of the TCAs while waiting for relief of their depression. Compliance with treatment with the newer antidepressants is much less of a problem and the chances of a response are therefore considerably enhanced.

As well as being more acceptable to patients the newer antidepressants are safer then the older TCAs. The anticholinergic effects and problems of cardiotoxicity of the TCAs have been largely avoided in the newer antidepressants and this makes them more safely available than the older TCAs for a wide range of patients.

'ATYPICAL' ANTIDEPRESSANTS

The mechanism of action of some of the newer antidepressants which include mianserin, trazadone and viloxazine appeared to be different from the TCAs and they became known as 'second generation antidepressants' to distinguish them from the earlier compounds. The TCAs were thought to exert their antidepressant effect by blocking the re-uptake of the neurotransmitters, noradrenaline and serotonin at the synapse but certain compounds which have antidepressant efficacy did not fit this model and therefore came to be known as 'atypical' antidepressants.

Mianserin

Mianserin was the first antidepressant introduced with a completely novel mechanism of action. It has antagonising effects on α_2 receptors and on 5-HT_1, 5-HT_2, and 5-HT_3 receptors and this was seen to be an effective combination which has stimulated the development of a range of potential new antidepressants. Mianserin was found to be effective both in depression and in anxiety. Initially its efficacy in anxiety was attributed to its sedative properties but it now appears that the 5-HT receptor antagonism is more important. The recommended dose of mianserin is 60 mg daily although higher and lower doses are used. Doubts about the efficacy of mianserin, particularly in the low dose of 30 mg, have been allayed by recent placebo-controlled studies showing efficacy of the same order as the TCAs and newer antidepressants.[1,2] Mianserin has the advantage of improved safety in overdose which makes it particularly suitable for those at risk of suicide. This advantage has to be weighed against reports of blood dyscrasias, particularly in the elderly, which appear to be at a level which appears slightly higher than is seen with TCAs, namely in about one per 8000 prescriptions. In the UK regular blood monitoring is recommended early in treatment.

Mianserin does not produce anticholinergic effects and shows an ability to reverse some of these effects which makes it the antidepressant of choice in patients with glaucoma, and in those with urinary hesitancy.

Trazadone

Trazadone was the first of the new generation of safe antidepressants to be made available in the USA but its success there has not been paralleled by an easy acceptance in Europe where it has had to compete with a range of new antidepressants. The α_1 receptor antagonism that is one of trazadone's pharmacological actions has led to reports of priapism, a painful condition, which, in rare cases, led to surgical intervention. This drawback has caused some hesitation in prescribing for male patients.

Viloxazine

Viloxazine has noradrenaline uptake blocking effects and a weak effect on the serotonergic system. Evidence of its effectiveness is much lighter than with other newer antidepressants. Its relative failure in the UK and ready acceptance in France and Italy reveals more about marketing techniques than intrinsic efficacy. The nausea seen as a side effect must contribute to the excellent record of safety in overdosage. The relative lack of epileptogenic potential makes this the antidepressant of choice in treating depression in epileptic patients although caution is needed because of a possible drug interaction with phenytoin.

ANTIDEPRESSANTS IN SPECIAL SITUATIONS

Epilepsy and depression

Treating depression in patients with epilepsy is problematic because of the risk of antidepressants reducing the control of seizures. Seizures are reported during treatment with nearly all antidepressants though they seem to be more frequent with the older TCAs. It is quite difficult to obtain reliable data on the incidence of convulsions associated with antidepressants from spontaneous reporting systems since there is considerable underreporting particularly with older TCAs where the association is accepted. The most reliable data available comes from studies before the individual drugs were released. All of the tricyclic antidepressants are associated with an increased incidence of convulsions. The incidence is dose related and occurs in about 1–2% with high doses of imipramine, clomipramine, amitriptyline and maprotiline for example. It is acknowledged that all widely used antidepressants are associated with some risk of increased convulsions and the maximum acceptable rate for an antidepressant is taken as 0.5%. For this reason tricyclics should be used cautiously and should not be used in patients with a previous history of fits. The incidence of fits with the newer antidepressants is somewhat lower: the incidence with fluvoxamine and fluoxetine is reported as 0.2% in the clinical trials, and mianserin and trazadone are associated with a slightly higher rate.

The only antidepressant which does not seem to be associated with increased convulsions is viloxazine and it should therefore be regarded as the antidepressant of choice.

Glaucoma and urinary retention in depression

The TCAs have marked anticholinergic effects which are likely to precipitate glaucoma and urinary retention in those who are susceptible. Antidepressants which are not associated with much in the way of anticholinergic effects such as fluoxetine, fluvoxamine, viloxazine and possibly trazadone should be preferred. However the treatment of choice should be mianserin which has been shown to have a positive effect on urinary flow.

Recent myocardial infarction

One of the most common problems encountered with the older TCAs is cardiotoxicity, some measure of which may be gained from the figures of lethality following overdose. Though these effects in therapeutic dosage given to healthy individuals might not be of particular clinical importance, in the depressed population, many of whom are in the older age group and likely to be at risk of undetected heart disease, these effects are an important consideration. It is obviously important to avoid prescribing the older TCAs for patients who have angina or recent myocardial incidents. From the overdose data the safest antidepressants appear to be lofepramine and mianserin, the latter having been investigated for safety specifically in patients with myocardial infarct.[3] The pharmacology of the 5-HT uptake inhibitors suggests that these antidepressants will also be appropriate for patients with impaired cardiac function.

ADVERSE DRUG REACTIONS WITH ANTIDEPRESSANTS IN NORMAL USAGE VERSUS OVERDOSE

Serious adverse drug reactions, including hepatotoxicity, rash, urticaria and agranulocytosis, are reported with all the older psychotropic drugs. They are also reported with the newer antidepressants since, in spite of the more stringent assessment procedures for new antidepressants before they reach the market, the rarity of these unpredictable events means that they may not occur even in an extensive testing programme. Agranulocytosis, which is reported with many of the older TCAs, particularly imipramine,[4,5] is also seen with mianserin at a slightly higher level than the TCAs.[6] Blood dyscrasias, as would be expected, occur more frequently in the elderly, a group in which mianserin has been preferentially used because of the safety of its cardiovascular profile. There have been reports of priapism with trazadone,[7] and, more recently, an update on adverse drug reactions issued from the Committee on Safety of Medicines has warned of liver function abnormalities with lofepramine.[8] These are however rare events and the incidence of serious adverse reactions appears in general to be very low with antidepressants (Table 5.1).

Table 5.1. Adverse drug reactions and deaths from overdose with antidepressants.

Drug	Fatal ADRs per million prescriptions	Death from overdose per million prescriptions
Dothiepin	<1	50.0
Amitriptyline	<1	46.5
Nortriptyline	1–2	39.2
Maprotiline	<1	37.6
Doxepin	<1	31.3
Imipramine	1–2	28.4
Trimipramine	<1	27.6
Clomipramine	5	11.1
Mianserin	2–3	5.6

Figures for ADRs taken from CSM Update 1985;[6] deaths from overdose from Cassidy and Henry, 1987.[9]

In our concern to reduce this type of risk we should not overlook the fact that far more deaths are caused by overdose with antidepressants than by adverse drug adverse reactions. The choice of an antidepressant to reduce the risk of adverse effects to the patient has to take the risk associated with overdose into account in an illness such as depression where the risk of a suicide attempt is acknowledged to be high. There is a rational basis for choice of antidepressant since the figures of deaths from overdose with

Table 5.2. Profile of side effects of newer antidepressants.

	Anticholinergic side effects	Cardiotoxicity	Safety in overdose
Newer TCAs			
Dothiepin	Risk	Risk	Risk
Doxepin	Risk	Risk	Risk
Maprotiline	Risk	Risk	Risk
Lofepramine	Safe	Safe	Safe
'Atypical' antidepressants			
Mianserin	Safe	Safe	Safe
Trazadone	Safe	Safe	Safe
Viloxazine	Safe	Safe	Safe
5-HT uptake inhibitors			
Fluvoxamine	Safe	Safe	Safe
Fluoxetine	Safe	Safe	Safe

different antidepressants are relatively consistent (see Chapter 12) Those newer antidepressants that have reached wide usage are overwhelmingly safer than the older TCAs in overdosage and should therefore be the first choice of treatment (Table 5.2).

OTHER PHARMACOLOGICAL TREATMENTS

Flupenthixol

There is some evidence that flupenthixol has antidepressant properties particularly in low doses. The placebo-controlled evidence in major depression is however rather light and concerns about neurological complications and the possibility of movement disorders developing have dampened enthusiasm. Low doses of flupenthixol are however probably effective in recurrent brief depressions and in the mood disturbances seen in borderline personalities.

Tryptophan

The formal evidence of the antidepressant effect of tryptophan on its own is weak and contradictory. This is a pity as there is considerable prejudice in some patients against drugs and a valid dietary approach is attractive. There is rather better evidence that tryptophan given as an adjunct to low doses of TCAs such as amitriptyline will improve the antidepressant response. Adding tryptophan to standard doses of antidepressants has been used in resistant depression although this has not been adequately tested. The approach is not without its dangers. There have been reports of movement disorders arising during treatment with tryptophan in combination with potent 5-HT uptake inhibitors. Some 1500 cases of eosinophilia myalgia syndrome (EMS) with 13 deaths have been reported in the USA associated with tryptophan as a dietary supplement which has led to its withdrawal in most countries. Expert opinion suggests that EMS is attributable to a recent contaminant in the manufacture of tryptophan.

Lithium

Some studies have found lithium to possess direct antidepressant properties but none have established efficacy equivalent to recognised antidepressants. There is more convincing evidence that lithium when added to conventional antidepressants may help to obtain extra response in resistant depression, but this approach carries a risk of drug interactions.[10]

Lithium has a more orthodox role in the prophylaxis of bipolar depression where it remains the agent of choice. The evidence of its ability to prolong the periods of remission and diminish the severity of the subsequent depression or mania is convincing. The evidence for the use of lithium in unipolar illness is less well documented and there are alternatives which are easier to use and which have fewer side effects.

The toxic level and the therapeutic level of lithium are close and toxic confusional states, coma and death have been reported with levels as low as 1.5 mmol/l. The level of lithium in plasma needs to be kept as close to 0.5–0.6 mmol/l as possible and only raised in those who have been shown not to respond at the lower levels. Lithium is usually prescribed in slow-release preparations and the dose is adjusted to achieve appropriate plasma levels. Slightly higher levels may be required in individual patients but the risks of side effects are increased. There has been justified concern about renal toxicity with microscopic tubular necrosis, polyuria and polydipsia. Hypothyroidism, weight gain and tremor are not uncommon. Because of fears of teratogenicity lithium should be discontinued well before considering pregnancy.

Benzodiazepines as antidepressants

Alprazolam

The introduction of benzodiazepine derivatives for the treatment of depression is a new approach in the development of antidepressants. Alprazolam is the only one of this class to claim efficacy although this is disputed.

There is considerable concern among clinicians about the wisdom of using benzodiazepines for the treatment of depression because of the possibility of dependence developing. The advice of the Royal College of Psychiatrists on the best use of benzodiazepines is for rapid symptomatic relief in anxiety in very short courses of treatment lasting no longer than 4 weeks.[11] Depression on the other hand is a long term illness which requires treatment for many months to ensure complete resolution. This requirement should discourage treatment with benzodiazepines because of the increased risk of dependence with time. With this in mind it seems unwise to develop benzodiazepine compounds as antidepressants unless there is both clear evidence of antidepressant efficacy and that the problem of dependence has been overcome.

Alprazolam has been investigated as an antidepressant but considerable doubts are entertained about the claims that have been made for its efficacy. It is felt that evidence of efficacy on the core symptoms or in clearly defined depression has not been established. For this reason its indications have been limited to anxiety disorders where there is adequate evidence of efficacy.

It also seems that the fears about dependence developing in depressed patients treated with alprazolam were justified in view of the increasing

Table 5.3.   Benzodiazepines in depression.

1. Disinhibition of suicidal acts reported
2. Benzodiazepines associated with tolerance and dependence except in short courses
3. Treatment of depression should persist over 4–6 months, but benzodiazepines should only be used for short courses, maximum 4 weeks
4. Benzodiazepines should not be used without a proven antidepressant

number of reports of withdrawal problems with this drug.[12] Other properties of benzodiazepines which make them of doubtful value in depression, for example a certain disinhibiting effect,[13] have also not been avoided with alprazolam. The report of a significant increase in aggression and suicidal behaviour during treatment with alprazolam compared with placebo which was attributed to this effect is disquieting in view of the risk of suicide attempts in depressed patients. Table 5.3 shows the main points which should be considered before benzodiazepines are prescribed in depression.

REFERENCES

1. Branconnier R.J., Cole J.O. and Ghazzinian S. (1981). The therapeutic profile of mianserin in mild elderly depressives. In: *Typical and Atypical Antidepressants* (Ed. E. Costa and G. Racagni), Raven Press, New York.
2. Muijen M., Roy D., Silverstone T., Mehmet A. and Christie M. (1988). A comparative clinical trial of fluoxetine, mianserin and placebo with depressed outpatients. *Acta Psychiatrica Scandinavica*, **75**, 384–390.
3. Kopera H. (1978). Antidepressants in cardiac patients. In: *Stress and the Heart* (Ed. D. Wheatley), Raven Press, New York, pp. 191–205.
4. Albertini R.S. and Penders T.M. (1978). Agranulocytosis associated with tricyclics. *Journal of Clinical Psychiatry*, **39**, 483–485.
5. Vincent P.C. (1986). Drug-induced aplastic anaemia and agranulocytosis. Incidence and mechanisms. *Drugs*, **31**, 52–63.
6. Committee on Safety of Medicines (1985). Adverse reactions to antidepressants. *British Medical Journal*, **291**, 1638.
7. Coccaro E.F. and Siever L.J. (1985). Second generation antidepressants: A comparative review. *Journal of Clinical Pharmacology*, **25**, 241–260.
8. Committee on Safety of Medicines (1988). Lofepramine (Gamanil) and abnormal tests of liver function. *Current Problems*, **23**.
9. Cassidy S. and Henry J. (1987). Fatal toxicity of antidepressant drugs in overdose. *British Medical Journal*, **295**, 1021–1024.
10. Committee on Safety of Medicines (1988). Fluvoxamine (Faverin): adverse reaction profile. *Current Problems*, **22**.
11. Priest R.G. and Montgomery S.A. (1988). Benzodiazepines and dependence. *Royal College of Psychiatrists Bulletin*, **12**, 107–109.
12. Juergens S.M. and Morse R.M. (1988). Alprazolam dependence in seven patients. *American Journal of Psychiatry*, **145**, 625–627.
13. Gardner D.L. and Cowdry R.W. (1985). Alprazolam-induced dyscontrol in borderline personality disorder. *American Journal of Psychiatry*, **141**, 98–100.

6

5-HT Uptake Inhibitors

There have been a number of approaches to the development of new, improved antidepressants but the one that has been arguably the most productive in bringing new antidepressants into clinical practice has concentrated on drugs which affect the serotonin system. The focus on this class of compound was encouraged by the hypothesis that serotonin was particularly involved in changes in mood and that drugs which potentiate serotonin might therefore be more effective antidepressants. The hypothesis was in tune with clinical findings which indicated that a dysfunction of 5-HT metabolism, manifest in lowered levels of 5-hydroxyindoleacetic acid (5-HIAA) in cerebrospinal fluid (CSF), was associated with depression. This dysfunction was not apparent in all depressed patients and the existence of a subgroup of 'serotonin depression' was postulated.[1, 2] One way of improving the treatment of depression, it seemed, would be to use an antidepressant which acted specifically on the serotonin system in patients whose depression was characterised by a serotonin disturbance.

The test of the hypothesis had to await the development of drugs with a specific and selective effect on serotonin. Some of the early tricyclic antidepressants (TCAs) had serotonergic effects but also had substantial effects on a wide range of other systems, including effects on cholinergic, muscarinic receptors etc. Many of these pharmacological actions were involved in the unpleasant side effects associated with TCA treatment and it was natural to develop drugs with more specific pharmacological actions to avoid some of these unwanted effects.

EFFICACY OF 5-HT UPTAKE INHIBITORS

We knew a good deal more about the new 5-HT uptake inhibitors when they reached clinical use than has been the case in the past with new drugs because of the increased stringency of drug assessment now in force. In the European Community the Committee on Proprietary Medicinal Products (CPMP) has issued guidelines for the conduct of studies to assess antidepressant efficacy which increase the reliability of efficacy findings in clinical trials. These guidelines stress the need to assess efficacy in the syndrome of depression not just on symptoms, and emphasise that efficacy needs to be judged in placebo-controlled studies. They also formalise what has come to be regarded as good methodological practice with requirements of an adequate assessment period, properly defined depression of adequate severity, the use of appropriate instruments of assessment, etc. As a result we have quite a clear idea of the level of efficacy of new antidepressants as they are introduced. This is true of the new 5-HT uptake inhibitors which have been subjected to extensive testing in placebo-controlled trials in large numbers of patients before being released for general use. Their advantages, as well as any shortcomings, are consequently well known.

Fluoxetine, fluvoxamine, and citalopram, have all reached the market in some European countries and/or in N. America and they will probably be followed shortly by paroxetine and sertraline. An overview of the clinical trials in this class of compound shows that 5-HT uptake inhibitors are clearly effective in major depression. As is to be expected in a very extensive clinical trial programme there are some studies where the strength of the efficacy findings is less marked and some where it is more marked.

The hope that 5-HT uptake inhibitors might prove to be more effective in depression than the TCAs has not been fulfilled. The overall conclusion is that the 5-HT uptake inhibitors are effective as antidepressants in a broad range of depressed patients and are of the same order of efficacy as the TCAs. To establish the equal efficacy of two active antidepressants in a clinical trial requires very large numbers of patients because of the small differences in response that could be expected and the individual comparisons of 5-HT uptake inhibitors with TCAs have mostly been too small. It is however possible to get some idea of the relative efficacy of those 5-HT uptake inhibitors which have been comprehensively tested in clinical trials by analysing the combined data of the studies which have included a TCA treatment group. The impression from an analysis of this kind with fluoxetine, fluvoxamine, paroxetine and sertraline for example, suggests efficacy of the same order as the TCAs and this is likely to apply to other compounds as well.

It is to some extent surprising that efficacy could be so readily established with the 5-HT uptake inhibitors in comparison with TCAs since the most frequently used assessment measure in the clinical trials, the Hamilton Rating Scale for depression, carries something of a bias against them. On this scale some of the side effects which are characteristic of 5-HT uptake inhibitors, for example weight loss, gastrointestinal effects, some increased anxiety, would contribute to a rating of severity of depression. Moreover the 5-HT uptake inhibitors generally lack the sedative effects of the older TCAs and this would also register on the Hamilton Scale as a disadvantage.

SIDE EFFECTS OF 5-HT UPTAKE INHIBITORS

The 5-HT uptake inhibitors are undoubtedly better tolerated and more acceptable to patients than the older TCAs. The clinical studies are consistent in finding that the 5-HT uptake inhibitors are associated with fewer unwanted effects than the TCAs with which they have been compared and, although there are some differences between compounds, the level of side effects with many of these new antidepressants is not very different from that seen with placebo. In general the 5-HT uptake inhibitors have few of the anticholinergic effects which limit treatment with the TCAs, they lack the cardiotoxic effects of the TCAs and are therefore probably relatively safe in overdose. They are not sedative which makes them a useful treatment for patients who are trying to continue at work or to drive cars.

Nervousness

Their characteristic side effects, expected from the pharmacology, relate to anxiety and gastrointestinal disturbance. Varying amounts of nervousness, anxiety or agitation, reported with all 5-HT uptake inhibitors, occur in some patients early in treatment but generally subside rapidly. Contrary to expectation this effect does not usually appear to compromise treatment even in patients where there is a prominent anxiety component. The anxiety symptoms are seen to respond well to treatment with a number of the 5-HT uptake inhibitors and some studies have even shown an improved response in these symptoms compared with treatment with TCAs.[3-5]

Nausea and weight loss

The gastrointestinal effects vary from mild discomfort, nausea, weight loss, to in extreme cases vomiting. The weight loss, which is persistent and appears to occur with most 5-HT uptake inhibitors, occurs most in the heaviest patients and is not seen to be a significant clinical problem. This side effect may indeed be welcome in some depressed patients who complain of putting on weight during treatment with TCAs. It is likely that some 5-HT uptake inhibitors may be used in higher doses in the treatment of obesity. The amount of nausea experienced by patients during treatment with 5-HT uptake inhibitors varies from compound to compound and may well be related to the dose as it appears more obvious with higher doses.

CHOOSING THE RIGHT DOSE

It is unfortunate that there are not better means of establishing the appropriate dose before a new antidepressant is introduced onto the market as it is possible that useful drugs could be lost because too high a dose is selected as the standard. The choice of dose is often based on dose ranging studies in which the dose is raised until an effect is seen. These studies carry an inherent bias towards the choice of higher doses although in clinical usage these may not turn out to be the most useful. For example the early studies with fluoxetine used a dose of 60–80 mg but later fixed dose studies found efficacy at the lower dose of 20 mg with a better balance of side effects to efficacy.[6,7] It is possible therefore that nausea which seems to be more often reported with fluvoxamine than some other 5-HT uptake inhibitors may be a problem because the recommended standard dose of fluvoxamine is too high.

FLUOXETINE

Fluoxetine has rather specific 5-HT uptake inhibiting effects. Its active metabolite, norfluoxetine, has a very long half-life of about 10 days which has both disadvantages and advantages. The long half-life allows intermittent treatment to be considered and also conveys advantages in overcoming problems of compliance, particularly in long-term treatment. A level of the drug in plasma continues to be maintained even if patients are erratic in taking medication. The disadvantage is that abrupt withdrawal of the drug, should it be needed with serious adverse drug reactions for example, is not possible. If treatment with an MAOI is considered, a long interval should be left between treatments to avoid dangerous interreactions.

The efficacy of fluoxetine in the treatment of the acute episode, and also in longer-term maintenance treatment and in the prophylactic treatment of recurrent depression is convincing.[8] The placebo-controlled studies have shown that the preferred dose, at 20 mg, is lower than the early studies suggested.

The lack of anticholinergic effects suggests that compliance with treatment will be improved compared with the older TCAs. Initially nausea, nervousness and sleep disturbance may be seen in some patients but these seem to be transient.

FLUVOXAMINE

Fluvoxamine has been less thoroughly investigated than fluoxetine but it has good evidence of efficacy in major depression. Its profile of side effects is similar to other 5-HT uptake inhibitors but it appears to produce more nausea and vomiting than others. This may be related to the compound itself or to the use of the high dose established as effective in early studies. This early choice of dose has unfortunately not been subjected to fixed dose blinded trials to establish the lowest effective dose, which is thought to be much lower than the marketed recommended dose. Nausea may be tolerated but vomiting often is not; it compromises treatment and can sometimes be dangerous.

The good efficacy in obsessive compulsive disorder seen in three placebo-controlled trials[9-11] makes this the preferred treatment for this condition and it is probably more acceptable to patients than clomipramine which has marked anticholinergic effects as well as having a rather high rate of convulsions.

5-HT UPTAKE INHIBITORS FOR PARTICULAR GROUPS OF DEPRESSED PATIENTS

Patients sometimes fail to respond to one antidepressant but subsequently respond to treatment with another. It would clearly be helpful if there were rational guidelines for selecting a particular antidepressant for an individual patient in order to maximise response. The hope that 5-HT uptake inhibitors might prove to be a specific treatment for patients with a dysfunction in the serotonin system was dispelled by studies which compared the response of such patients to 5-HT uptake inhibitors or to antidepressants with a selective effect on the noradrenaline system.[12] Any selective clinical effect was overwhelmed by the general antidepressant effect of the drugs regardless of which neurotransmitter they affected.

There are however some aspects of the profile of action of the 5-HT uptake inhibitors which may make them particularly appropriate for certain kinds of patient.

Obsessive compulsive disorder

Patients with obsessive compulsive disorder (OCD) respond to clomipramine which has potent, although not exclusive, serotonergic effects but do not respond to other TCAs. The depression associated with OCD responds poorly to TCAs with the exception of clomipramine. Consistently, small studies in OCD have reported a selective advantage of 5-HT uptake inhibitors such as fluvoxamine and clomipramine over other antidepressants. The relative absence of a placebo response in OCD and the almost immediate and steady response of OCD to 5-HT uptake inhibitors is one of the strongest findings in the depression literature with all nine of the published placebo-controlled studies of clomipramine and all three of the placebo-controlled studies of fluvoxamine reporting efficacy (see Chapter 9). This effect appears independently of whether there is co-existing depression or not, or indeed whether other less well-established treatments such as behaviour therapy are used at the same time or not. The results from the recent as yet unpublished studies of other 5-HT uptake inhibitors are promising and suggest that 5-HT uptake inhibitors as a class will prove specifically useful in this indication.

Agitated depression

Increased nervousness and anxiety, which may be quite marked in some patients, is seen early in treatment with 5-HT uptake inhibitors and this has prompted the understandable concern that these antidepressants may be less useful in the treatment of agitated depression. It has also been commonly believed that the sedative effect of older TCAs such as amitriptyline was required for the treatment of agitated patients. Physicians have initially had some reservations about the use of 5-HT uptake inhibitors in agitated depression because they differ in this respect from the earlier TCAs as they are not sedative drugs.

These worries have been allayed by a number of metanalyses that have been made in the efficacy studies of the different 5-HT uptake inhibitors compared with reference TCAs and placebo, which consider the response of patients with agitated depression separately from those without. With fluoxetine, 17.5% of the total pool of patients included in studies were found to have moderate or severe degrees of agitation on entry to the studies and the response of these agitated depressed patients to fluoxetine was significantly better than to the comparator TCA or to placebo. A similar advantage for fluoxetine was seen in those depressed patients identified as suffering from marked degrees of anxiety prior to starting treatment.[3] A similar result is seen in an analysis of patients treated with fluvoxamine compared with imipramine.[13] The earlier 5-HT uptake inhibitor, zimelidine, was shown to have a significant advantage in treating the anxiety symptoms associated with depression when compared with the reference tricyclic antidepressant, amitriptyline,[4] and similar findings are reported with other new 5-HT uptake inhibitors.

In this context it is interesting to note the successful use of 5-HT uptake inhibitors in patients with a variety of anxiety disorders. Patients described as suffering from panic disorder were reported to be successfully treated with zimelidine[14,15] and there are positive results with fluvoxamine,[16] where the 5-HT uptake inhibitor showed a selective advantage in panic disorder compared with the noradrenaline uptake inhibitor, maprotiline.

These findings challenge the notion that a sedative tricyclic is the treatment of choice where anxiety symptoms are a prominent feature of depression.

This practice appears to be outmoded since fluvoxamine and fluoxetine, and possibly other 5-HT uptake inhibitors, are particularly effective in anxious or agitated depression compared with TCAs. The sedation with TCAs appears to have little therapeutic benefit compared with 5-HT uptake inhibitors and may even be counterproductive. It seems reasonable to suggest that 5-HT uptake inhibitors may turn out to be the preferred treatment in anxious or agitated depression.

Suicidal thoughts and acts

An association between a disturbance of serotonin metabolism and suicidal behaviour has been reported both in depressed patients and in personality disorder[17-21] and an intriguing possibility is that 5-HT uptake inhibitors might be more helpful than some other antidepressants in patients with suicidal thoughts. Independent studies have reported a differential improvement of suicidal thoughts early in treatment with several different antidepressants of this class, including fluoxetine, fluvoxamine, citalopram, and the earlier drug zimelidine which was withdrawn.[4,13,22,23] A metanalysis of the outcome of those patients considered 'at risk' of suicide with high initial scores on the suicide item of the Hamilton Rating Scale (HRS) showed that these patients had a better response to fluvoxamine than on either placebo or a reference TCA.[13] It is not known whether 5-HT uptake inhibitors would reduce suicide attempts as well and it would be difficult, but not impossible, to conduct a study to test this hypothesis. Some support for this idea is provided by the low level of deaths from overdose with clomipramine compared with other TCAs. The new 5-HT uptake inhibitors appear to be relatively safe in overdose, though the overdose data on these antidepressants are still limited.

Resistant depression

Clinicians who have focused on those patients who do not respond to TCAs or other antidepressants have suggested that drugs or combinations of drugs which aim to increase serotonergic function may be effective where others have failed although the trials on such combinations are not adequate. The number of patients who fail to respond to vigorous treatment continued over an adequate period of time are relatively few in number but form a worrying group for psychiatrists. Efficacy testing in resistant depression is not usually included in the early assessment of efficacy of a potential antidepressant and it is too soon therefore to say whether the new 5-HT uptake inhibitors will have a specific role in treating these patients. Reports of treatment with paroxetine of patients with true resistant depression are, however, promising and further research in this area is needed.

5-HT UPTAKE INHIBITORS—A SUMMARY

The evidence for the efficacy of the new 5-HT uptake inhibitors is now stronger for some of these compounds than for many existing antidepressants introduced in earlier years. The relative lack of side effects compared with TCAs, particularly the anticholinergic symptoms, make these compounds much easier to tolerate than the TCAs and would be expected to be associated with better compliance with treatment. The nausea, nervousness, and sleep disturbance reported in early clinical trials were found to be largely avoided when the dose was titrated downwards without loss of efficacy. The extra nausea and vomiting seen with fluvoxamine compared with some other 5-HT uptake inhibitors may well relate to being prescribed at too high a dose.

The incidence of serious adverse drug reactions is low when compared with TCAs and there is little cardiotoxicity and few convulsions. Reports of hepatotoxicity, blood dyscrasias and skin reactions suggest that these problems will occur with 5-HT uptake inhibitors at levels below or close to those seen with TCAs. The most dangerous reaction seen with 5-HT uptake inhibitors thus far is the fatal interaction reported with treatment following MAOIs. The interaction, which produces a hyperpyrexia, may be sudden in onset and seems most likely when a 5-HT uptake inhibitor is added to the treatment without a sufficient interval after stopping MAOIs. Similar interactions have been reported between lithium and 5-HT uptake inhibitors and between lithium and neuroleptics and have been classified as neuroleptic malignant syndrome.

The evidence of safety in overdose is difficult to assess until antidepressants have been in sufficiently wide usage; however the safety record of fluoxetine and fluvoxamine is very good and both drugs appear to be relatively safe in overdosage with a level of safety similar to lofepramine and mianserin.

REFERENCES

1. Asberg M., Thoren P., Traskman L., Bertilsson L. and Ringberger W. (1976). Serotonin depression: a biochemical subgroup within the affective disorders? *Science*, **191**, 478–480.
2. van Praag H.M., Korf J. and Schut T. (1973). Cerebral monoamines and depression. *Archives of General Psychiatry*, **28**, 827–830.
3. Montgomery S.A. (1989). The efficacy of fluoxetine as an antidepressant in the short and long term. *International Clinical Psychopharmacology*, **4** (S1), 113–119.
4. Montgomery S.A., McAuley R., Rani S.J., Roy D. and Montgomery D.B. (1981). A double blind comparison of zimelidine and amitriptyline in endogenous depression. *Acta Psychiatrica Scandinavica*, **63** (Suppl. 290), 314–327.
5. Fabre L.F. (1988). Study of paroxetine, imipramine and placebo in the treatment of depressed outpatients. *Psychopharmacology*, **96** (Suppl. 211).
6. Wernicke J.F., Dunlop S.R., Dornseif B.E. and Zerbe R.L. (1987). Fixed-dose fluoxetine therapy for depression. *Psychopharmacological Bulletin*, **23**, 164–168.

7. Wernicke J.F., Dunlop S.R., Dornseif B.E. and Bosomworth J.C. (1988). Low dose fluoxetine therapy for depression. *Psychopharmacology Bulletin*, **24**, 183–188.

8. Montgomery S.A., Dufour H., Brion S., Gailledreau J., Laqueille X., Ferrey G., Moron P., Parant-Lucena N., Singer L., Danion J.M., Beuzen J.N. and Pierredon M.A. (1988). The prophylactic efficacy of fluoxetine in unipolar depression. *British Journal of Psychiatry*, **153** (Suppl. 3), 69–76.

9. Goodman W.K., Price L.H., Rassmussen S.A., Delgado P.L., Heninger G.R. and Charney D.S. (1989). Efficacy of fluvoxamine in obsessive compulsive disorder, a double blind comparison with placebo. *Archives of General Psychiatry*, **46**, 36–43.

10. Perse T.L., Greist J., Jefferson J., Rosenfeld R. and Dar R. (1987). Fluvoxamine treatment of obsessive compulsive disorder. *American Journal of Psychiatry*, **144**, 1543–1548.

11. Price L., Goodman W., Charney D., Rasmussen S. and Heninger G. (1987). Treatment of severe obsessive compulsive disorder with fluvoxamine. *American Journal of Psychiatry*, **144**, 1059–1061.

12. Montgomery S.A., James D. and Montgomery D.B. (1987). Pharmacological specificity is not the same as clinical selectivity. In: *Clinical Pharmacology in Psychiatry* (Ed. S.G. Dahl, L.F. Gram, S.M. Paul and W.M. Potter), Springer, Berlin, pp. 179–183.

13. Wakelin J. (1988). The role of serotonin in depression and suicide. *Advances in Biological Psychiatry*, **17**, 70–83.

14. Evans L. and Moore G. (1981). The treatment of phobic anxiety by zimelidine. *Acta Psychiatrica Scandinavica*, **61** (Suppl. 290), 342–345.

15. Evans J., Kennedy L., Schneider P. and Hoey H. (1986). Effect of a selective serotonin uptake inhibitor in agoraphobia with panic attacks. *Acta Psychiatrica Scandinavica*, **73**, 49–53.

16. den Boer J.A. and Westenberg H.G.M. (1988). Effect of a serotonin and noradrenaline uptake inhibitor in panic disorder: a double-blind comparative study with fluvoxamine and maprotiline. *International Clinical Psychopharmacology*, **3**, 59–74.

17. Asberg M., Traskman L. and Thoren P. (1976). 5-HIAA in the cerebrospinal fluid—a biochemical suicide predictor? *Archives of General Psychiatry*, **33**, 1193–1197.

18. Montgomery S.A. and Montgomery D.B. (1982). Pharmacological prevention of suicidal behaviour. *Journal of Affective Disorders*, **4**, 291–298.

19. Banki C.M. and Arato M. (1983). Amine metabolites, neurendocrine findings and personality dimensions as correlates of suicidal behaviour. *Psychiatry Research*, **10**, 253–261.

20. Lopez-Ibor J.J., Saiz-Ruiz J. and Perez de los Cobos J.C. (1985). Biological correlations of suicide and aggressivity in major depressions with melancholia. *Neuropsychobiology*, **14**, 67–74.

21. Brown G.L., Ebert M.H., Goyer P.F., Jimerson D.C., Klein W.J., Bunney W.E. and Goodwin F.K. (1982). Aggression, suicide and serotonin; relationships to CSF amine metabolites. *American Journal Psychiatry*, **139**, 741–746.

22. Muijen M., Roy D., Silverstone T., Mehmet A. and Christie M. (1988). A comparative clinical trial of fluoxetine, mianserin and placebo with depressed outpatients. *Acta Psychiatrica Scandinavica*, **75**, 384–390.

23. de Wilde J., Mertens C., Fredricson Overo K. and Hepfner Petersen H.E. (1985). Citalopram versus mianserin, a controlled double-blind trial in depressed patients. *Acta Psychiatrica Scandinavica*, **72**, 89–96..

7

The Treatment of Anxiety

MILD ANXIETY

To treat or not to treat?

The management of the patient who presents with mild anxiety is a common problem for the practitioner who has to assess what is often a medley of small complaints. Patients may complain primarily of somatic symptoms such as palpitations, dry mouth, visual disturbances, or a variety of aches and pains, as much as, if not more than the psychic experiences of undue worrying and concern. They may have a variety of complaints or may focus on only one or two symptoms. It is in the nature of the condition that the fearful individual will fear the symptoms themselves and this worry will lead him to consult the doctor. The symptoms are often associated with stress and are usually transient, resolving as the circumstances change or with appropriate adjustment on the part of the patient.

Reassurance for mild anxiety

Mild anxiety symptoms usually respond to simple reassurance whether self administered by the insightful individual or reinforced in the clinic. Clearly there is little time in the busy surgery for sophisticated behavioural relearning techniques aimed at overcoming maladaptive behaviours. Simple counselling, individually or in groups, appears to be helpful and can be provided by nurses, psychologists and other non-medical colleagues as well as by the medical practitioner.

The busy practitioner who has to try to keep within the format of the usual brief consultation might find it easier to use the technique of the extended interview asking the patient to return for a further discussion intermittently over several clinic visits. This has the great advantage of allowing time to pass while providing a supportive and reassuring context. The traditional role of a doctor in facing minor symptomatology which is quite likely to evaporate is to provide reassurance while seeing whether a treatable illness emerges. In many cases it will not and reassurance and therapeutic listening will have been sufficient. If, however, symptoms of an underlying illness emerge, this assessment period will have provided the opportunity for its early recognition.

Drugs in mild anxiety

Are they effective?

There seems little justification for using an anxiolytic drug for mild anxiety unless it is effective and safe. The evidence for the efficacy of anxiolytic drugs in this condition is not robust. While the benzodiazepines have been shown to be effective in reducing the symptoms of moderate and severe anxiety, the evidence of their efficacy in mild anxiety is weaker. In several studies which have included a comparison with a non-pharmacological treatment such as counselling, the cognitive treatment appears to be as good as treatment with a benzodiazepine.[1] Whether either treatment is better than no treatment is not clear in mild anxiety. All drugs are associated with some risks and there is good reason to avoid their use unless they are of proven efficacy. As we now know, the benzodiazepines, for example, are not as safe as originally thought and the long-term risks of treatment are likely to far outweigh any immediate benefit accruing to the patient from the relief of mild symptoms which would probably resolve with reassurance or with the passage of time.

Useful in sleep disturbance?

Sleep disturbance is a very common symptom that brings the anxious patient to the doctor's surgery and there is frequently quite strong pressure from patients for the doctor to provide symptomatic treatment. The efficacy of the benzodiazepines in alleviating insomnia has led to them being widely prescribed as hypnotics. The presence of mild sleep disturbance is, however, natural in certain circumstances and reassurance and advice on good sleep practices may be the most appropriate help (see Table 7.1). It is important to try to avoid the use of medication, which carries a potential for dependence, for a normal reaction which is likely to be transient. If the sleep disturbance is more prolonged, the pressure to prescribe increases but, since the risk of dependence is increased in patients with chronic sleep disturbance, initiating treatment with benzodiazepines should be avoided if possible.

Avoiding symptomatic treatment of insomnia with benzodiazepines does not, however, mean that it should be ignored. Sleep disturbance may be a

Table 7.1. Simple advice for improving sleep.

1. Avoid caffeine in afternoon, evening, or night, e.g. tea, coffee, chocolate, or cola drinks.

2. Postpone thinking about worrying issues within an hour of bedtime.

3. Drink warm milk-based drink before sleeping.

4. Prepare for bed with a relaxing bath, etc., before retiring.

5. Avoid rich food in the evening.

6. Read before sleeping. Novels have been produced for their sedative properties for longer than benzodiazepines!

7. Reduce alcohol intake. In older patients, especially, alcohol shortens sleep.

useful indicator not only of anxiety but also of an underlying, unrecognised depression and the possibility of the presence of other depressive symptomatology should be investigated.

A GUIDE FOR THE TREATMENT OF ANXIETY

An important reason for avoiding treatment with benzodiazepines for the symptomatic relief of anxiety symptoms is the risk that recognition of an underlying treatable illness may be delayed. As has been discussed elsewhere, anxiety symptoms may be a very prominent part of depressive illness and symptomatic treatment may reduce the overt anxiety, leaving the underlying depression untreated. In this way the illness may be prolonged or even exacerbated. There is ample evidence that in primary care patients with both kinds of symptoms are more likely to receive treatment for their anxiety with benzodiazepines than for their depression with antidepressants.[2,3] The presence of anxiety symptoms should always alert the general practitioner to the need to ask about depressive symptoms. In deciding on the treatment of the patient who presents with anxiety the physician will check:

1. Diagnosis—is there another illness, either physical or psychological?
2. Presence of depression which will need energetic treatment.
3. Severity—is there an illness or only mild symptoms which may resolve with reassurance.

Antidepressants in the treatment of anxiety

At the time of their introduction the benzodiazepines appeared to be safe drugs with a low level of associated dangerous side effects apart from the need for caution in situations where psychomotor impairment would be undesirable.[4,5] The recognition of the shortcomings of the benzodiazepines, which, although remarkably effective in the rapid short-term relief of anxiety symptoms, due to their potential for dependence do not provide an appropriate treatment for anxiety states which tend to be chronic conditions, has left the physician with the problem of knowing what pharmacological treatment to offer. Recent research into the use of antidepressants in conditions outside conventional depression appears to have provided an effective alternative. The efficacy of antidepressants in patients suffering from anxiety disorders has been established in a number of placebo-controlled studies. Patients with mixed anxiety and depression, with anxiety states, and with panic have all been studied and the antidepressants used have performed consistently well.

Mild anxiety and depression

A large group of patients suffering from anxiety, mixed anxiety and depression, but excluding patients with major depression, were treated in a Medical Research Council study with a benzodiazepine, an antidepressant or placebo.[6] The results were striking: the antidepressant was significantly superior to the placebo across the entire spectrum of patients. Even more interesting was the finding that the antidepressant was also superior to the benzodiazepine which itself was no different from placebo in the group as a whole. The benzodiazepine was effective only in a very small group of patients with severe anxiety symptoms.

Anxiety states

A more specific study which investigated the anxiety end of the spectrum[7] compared the response of 240 patients with anxiety states to imipramine, chlordiazepoxide and placebo. Although in this study response to the benzodiazepine was significantly improved compared with placebo, a better response was seen in the group treated with the antidepressant which was found to be significantly better than both the benzodiazepine and the placebo. Contrary to expectation imipramine exerted a more specifically anti-anxiety effect than chlordiazepoxide and this effect did not depend on the level of co-existing depression.

Panic disorder

The concept of panic as a separate illness within the anxiety disorders was encouraged by the finding that imipramine was effective in a group of patients complaining of predominantly panic symptoms.[8] Subsequent studies have confirmed the benefit of imipramine compared with placebo and benzodiaze-pines as well as of other antidepressants.[9,10] The characteristic delay in response to antidepressants seen in the treatment of depression is also seen in the treatment of anxiety and panic.

Relief of anxiety symptoms is undoubtedly more rapid with the benzodiazepines and studies with the new benzodiazepine, alprazolam, showed an early onset of action within the first 1–2 weeks.[11] In the controlled studies of alprazolam compared with an antidepressant this early advantage of the benzodiazepine is, however, not sustained and an antidepressant appears to be the more effective treatment overall. It seems that benzodiazepines might therefore be used to best effect in the initial treatment of the condition while awaiting the effect of the antidepressant to become apparent. If this approach is adopted it would be wise to use benzodiazepines for their rapid initial action only, and to stop them within 4 weeks to reduce the substantial risk of dependence. More recent studies point to the usefulness of non-sedating antidepressants given in low doses as the treatment of choice in panic disorder.[12]

One of the problems in assessing treatments for panic disorder has been the overlap between the substantial number of patients with panic disorder and concomitant depression and those without. Panic symptoms are found as a natural feature of major depression and one might suspect that the responsiveness of panic disorder with concomitant depression is due to the treatment of the depression with an antidepressant. This question was addressed in an interesting series of studies in patients suffering from panic who had low initial Hamilton Depression Scale ratings (less than 15). It was found that the noradrenaline re-uptake inhibitor, maprotiline, was associated with a very small response whereas the response to the 5-HT re-uptake inhibitor, fluvoxamine, was significantly better.[12] Since both drugs are established antidepressants it implies that antidepressants as a class are not necessarily effective in pure panic disorder but that antidepressants with a specific effect on serotonin may offer particularly appropriate treatment.

Practical considerations in the treatment of anxiety with antidepressants

Antidepressants are not only effective in the treatment of anxiety, it seems their overall efficacy is better than that of the benzodiazepines. In view of their lack of dependence potential antidepressants would therefore be the preferred treatment. There are nonetheless problems in their use in anxiety. They are slow to produce their effect and patients who have known the rapid relief obtained in the short term from benzodiazepines may need encouragement to persevere with treatment. Many of the studies, particularly in panic, report that patients find it difficult to tolerate antidepressants and discontinue treatment before any anxiolytic effect is obtained. Imipramine was noticed to produce irritability, insomnia and apprehension even in low doses in some panic patients and since these are patients who worry about symptoms these early effects can be a problem. A transient increase in anxiety in the early stages of treatment is seen with some of the newer 5-HT uptake inhibitors both in depression and in anxiety states. This phenomenon can be discouraging to patients particularly those with panic.

There is some comfort in the evidence that low doses of antidepressants can be effective, since unwanted side effects may be avoided in this way. The obvious procedure is to start with the lowest possible dose to minimise the paradoxical increase in anxiety in the first 24 hours and to raise the dose slowly. Since there is likely to be a delay in response to an antidepressant short courses of benzodiazepines, of say 2 weeks, may be used in the more severe anxiety cases for the early stages of treatment to help the patient while waiting for the antidepressant to exert its effect.

Choosing an antidepressant—Is a sedative or non-sedative antidepressant best?

Clinicians have traditionally used sedative drugs to control anxiety and it appears to have been assumed that the sedation was necessary for an anxiolytic effect. The early studies of the treatment of panic disorder, however, found better efficacy with antidepressants, such as imipramine, that are less sedative than others and the efficacy of newer non-sedative antidepressants in treating anxiety shows that a sedative effect is not a *sine qua non*.

Positive effects have also been seen in agoraphobia and panic disorder with zimelidine, a non-sedative 5-HT uptake inhibitor no longer available.[13,14] An apparently specific effect on anxiety has been reported with several of the newer 5-HT uptake inhibitors, e.g. fluvoxamine, fluoxetine, and zimelidine, which have consistently shown an advantage for the non-sedative 5-HT uptake inhibitors compared with the sedative TCA, amitriptyline, in reducing anxiety symptoms in depression.[15-17]

The difference in efficacy of sedative and non-sedative antidepressants is not entirely clear-cut since the sedative TCA, clomipramine, and the sedative serotonin antagonist, mianserin, appear to be effective even in small doses. Further studies are needed to clarify the issue but there is the possibility that the effect of both clomipramine and mianserin on serotonin may be the deciding factor in efficacy. The demonstration, in a study of panic disorder, of an advantage for fluvoxamine compared with maprotiline, an antidepressant affecting predominantly the noradrenergic system, suggests the intriguing possibility that the augmented response may be related to effects on the serotonin system.[12] As the evidence accumulates for the importance of the serotonin system in anxiety it would seem illogical to assume that the sedative effects of antidepressants, brought about largely through effects on histaminic receptors, should be necessary in reducing anxiety.

It is apparent that 5-HT uptake inhibitors and also 5-HT antagonists may have a particularly beneficial effect in anxiety. The exact role of 5-HT antagonists, for which there is evidence of efficacy in anxiety states and in depression, is still being investigated. A range of 5-HT_1, 5-HT_2 and 5-HT_3 antagonists is now being investigated for efficacy in treating both anxiety and depression and related serotonin disorders, such as migraine, eating disorders and possibly addiction, but it is still too early to say if important new treatments are likely to become available in the very near future.

The efficacy of antidepressants in treating anxiety is very welcome in view of the acknowledged difficulty of separating anxiety and depression and the unreliability of the distinction in general practice which has been shown in many studies. Faced with this dilemma it appears that doctors in primary care have adopted the idea that treatment takes precedence over diagnosis. In view of the wide spectrum of activity of antidepressants this may not be as foolish as it seems.

It is good practice to select a safe antidepressant in treating patients with panic symptoms because of the well documented link between suicide and panic disorder. The clear cut risk of suicide in patients with anxiety disorders[18] suggests that some of the older sedative tricyclic antidepressants should be avoided or used with great caution. Amitriptyline and dothiepin, for example, are associated with a higher rate of death from overdose than other available antidepressants and one of the newer safer antidepressants would therefore make a better choice of treatment.

Monoamine oxidase inhibitors

Early studies with the monoamine oxidase inhibitors (MAOIs), in heterogeneous groups of anxious patients, found these drugs to be effective in alleviating phobic and anxiety symptoms.[10] The patients included in the earlier studies were a mixed diagnostic group and it was suggested that MAOIs were also effective in what was called atypical depression. MAOIs, particularly phenelzine, which has been most extensively investigated, were also found to have efficacy in controlling panic attacks. More recently phenelzine has been shown to be as effective as imipramine in the treatment of panic attacks and its associated anxiety, and to be more effective on some symptoms. In view of the likely overlap between these categories of illness with major depression it is perhaps surprising that evidence of efficacy in major depression is relatively unconvincing and this implies that MAOIs may be effective in some kinds of depression but not others. The concept of atypical depression has been developed to try to define this group though treatment studies using this concept have had rather mixed results.

The dietary restrictions required in the use of this class of drugs limit their usefulness in anxiety disorders where safer drugs are available. There have been worrying reports of sudden death occurring from interactions with a range of drugs, some of them available without prescription over the counter, and caution is needed in selecting patients who will comply with warnings.

Other treatments

Alprazolam

Alprazolam is a triazolo-benzodiazepine with a different chemical structure to diazepam and its derivatives but sharing many of the pharmacological properties of those compounds. Its anxiolytic efficacy is established in the treatment of generalised anxiety and in the more severe manifestation of anxiety in panic disorder.[19,20] It appears to have a fairly rapid effect on anxiety symptoms and is initially well tolerated by patients. Clinicians have found it to be a useful treatment in panic disorder because it is pleasing to patients who may comply with treatment better than when treated with an antidepressant.

There are however drawbacks to this treatment. Reports have begun to appear of dependence problems in a sizeable minority of patients treated with alprazolam. Withdrawal phenomena similar to those seen with other benzodiazepines, including seizures[21,22] have also been reported following abrupt cessation of the drug. Some investigators have reported that panic attacks during gradual withdrawal of alprazolam appear to occur more rapidly, and are more of a problem than during withdrawal of an antidepressant. They have even suggested that cessation of alprazolam treatment may have the effect of increasing the frequency of subsequent panic attacks although controlled studies of withdrawal would be needed to confirm this.[22] In choosing a treatment the likelihood of dependence developing would have to be weighed against the possible therapeutic benefit. Both the Royal College of Psychiatrists and the Committee on Review of Medicines in the UK recommend stopping the treatment after no more than 2–4 weeks to avoid tolerance and dependence with all benzodiazepines.[23,24]

Buspirone

Buspirone hydrochloride has recently been introduced to provide an anxiolytic treatment which is not a benzodiazepine. The efficacy of buspirone in anxious patients is interesting since this drug is without significant sedative, cognitive, or anticonvulsant effects and does not appear to interfere with psychomotor function. Its clinical testing programme was based very largely on patients seen in primary care with anxious symptoms who are described as having generalised anxiety disorder.

One encouraging aspect of this drug is that, although it is still early days to be sure, there does not appear to be a risk of tolerance or dependence. At least one long-term study[25] has shown that higher doses were not required during maintenance treatment to sustain anxiolytic effect nor are withdrawal phenomena apparent during placebo-controlled withdrawal. If it is effective it would therefore be of considerable interest to the general practitioner. Unfortunately buspirone appears to have limitations. In some of the published studies there are reports that, although buspirone did not have unpleasant side effects apart from nausea, a substantial proportion of patients did not comply with treatment, some complaining of dysphoria. It seemed to be a mildly effective treatment for anxiety but did not make patients feel well quickly. There have not been extensive comparisons of buspirone with the non-sedative antidepressants which, being better tolerated, would be the preferred treatment in panic patients. However it is reported to be superior to placebo but rather less efficacious than imipramine in panic disorder.

Behaviour therapy

The emphasis of this review of treatment of the various categories of anxiety disorders has been on pharmacological treatments. This is inevitable since the efficacy of these treatments has been subjected to controlled testing and we can feel confident of the effects which have been demonstrated. It has proved much more difficult to find an adequate trial design to test the efficacy of behaviour therapy with a double blind neutral control.

In spite of this difficulty it is generally accepted that behaviour therapy is helpful in simple phobias. Anxiety is confined to a single feared situation which the individual increases and perpetuates by avoiding. Simple phobias are common and are found in some 12.5% of the normal population of whom only 2% present for treatment as in many cases the inconvenience is minor. These predictable and therefore avoidable fears respond well to behaviour therapy with controlled exposure which remains the treatment of choice and medication may not be needed. Opinion is more divided in the less clear cut conditions. One view is that behaviour therapy is the treatment of choice if there is accompanying avoidance behaviour as in agoraphobia.[26] Others are of the opinion that behaviour therapy can reduce phobic avoidance but does not alleviate panic attacks. Yet another approach is to use the effect of antidepressants in treating the panic attacks to also reduce the phobic avoidance. Antidepressant treatment may contribute to the patient's ability or willingness to comply with behavioural treatment programmes. There is no evidence that pharmacotherapy and behaviour therapy used together reduce the expected response and indeed the combination may enhance efficacy.[27]

Table 7.2.   A guide for the treatment of anxiety.

Determine severity	Consider possible treatment
Mild anxiety Minor increased nervousness, tension, panicky feelings, palpitations, dry mouth, sweating, choking, hyperventilation	• Self directed treatment, i.e. learning to cope • Life-style advice, i.e. not an illness • Therapeutic listening (labour intensive)
Moderate, severe or incapacitating anxiety Overwhelming panic, overwhelming anxiety, severe physical symptoms	• Extended interview • Anxiolytics covered by antidepressant

CONCLUSION

The classification of anxiety disorders is likely to be the subject of debate among psychiatrists for some time to come. From the practical point of view of treatment a simple classification based on what seems to be the most appropriate treatment will be most useful for practitioners (see Table 7.2).

REFERENCES

1. Catalan J., Gath D., Edmonds G. and Ennis J. (1984). The effects of non-prescribing of anxiolytics in general practice. *British Journal of Psychiatry*, **144**, 593–602.
2. Gullick E.L. and King L.J. (1979). Appropriateness of drugs prescribed by primary care physicians for depressed outpatients. *Journal of Affective Disorders*, **1**, 55–58 .
3. Weissman M.M. and Klerman G.L. (1977). The chronic depressive in the community: unrecognized and poorly treated. *Comprehensive Psychiatry*, **18**, 523–532.
4. Betts T.A., Clayton A.B. and Mackay G.M. (1972). Effects of four commonly used tranquillisers on low speed driving performance tests. *British Medical Journal*, **4**, 580–584.
5. Seppala T., Korttila K., Hakkinen S. and Linnoila M. (1976). Residual effects and skills related to driving after a single oral administration of diazepam, medazepam or lorazepam. *British Journal of Clinical Pharmacology*, **3**, 831–841 .
6. Johnstone E.C., Cunningham Owens D.G., Frith C.D., McPherson K., Dowie C., Riley G. and Gold A. (1980). Neurotic illness and its response to anxiolytic and antidepressant treatment. *Psychological Medicine*, **10**, 321–328.
7. Kahn R.J., McNair D.M., Lipman R.S., Covi L., Rickels K., Downing R., Fisher S. and Frankenthaler L.M. (1986). Imipramine and chlordiazepoxide in depressive and anxiety disorders II Efficacy in anxious out-patients. *Archives of General Psychiatry*, **43**, 79–85.
8. Klein D.F. and Fink M. (1962). Psychiatric reaction patterns to imipramine. *American Journal of Psychiatry*, **119**, 432–438.

9. Lydiard R.B. and Ballenger J.C. (1987). Antidepressants in panic disorder and agoraphobia. *Journal of Affective Disorders*, **13**, 153–168 .
10. Cassano G.B., Perugi G., McNair D.M. (1988). Panic disorder: review of the empirical and rational basis of pharmacological treatment. *Pharmacopsychiatry*, **21**, 157–165.
11. Liebowitz M.R., Fyer A.J., Gorman J.M., Campeas R., Levin A., Davies S.R., Goetz D. and Klein D.F. (1986). Alprazolam in the treatment of panic disorders. *Journal of Clinical Psychopharmacology*, **6**, 13–20.
12. den Boer J.A. and Westenberg H.G.M. (1988). Effect of a serotonin and noradrenaline uptake inhibitor in panic disorder. *International Clinical Psychopharmacology*, **3**, 59–74.
13. Evans L. and Moore G. (1981). The treatment of phobic anxiety by zimelidine. *Acta Psychiatrica Scandinavica*, **61** (Suppl. 290), 342–345.
14. Evans L., Kennardy J. and Schneider P. and Hoey H. (1986). Effect of a selective serotonin uptake inhibitor in agoraphobia with panic attacks. *Acta Psychiatrica Scandinavica*, **73**, 49–53.
15. Montgomery S. A., McAuley R., Rani S.J., Roy D. and Montgomery D.B. (1981). A double blind comparison of zimelidine and amitriptyline in endogenous depression. *Acta Psychiatrica Scandinavica*, **63** (Suppl. 290), 314–327.
16. Montgomery S.A. (1989). The efficacy of fluoxetine as an antidepressant in the short and long term. *International Clinical Psychopharmacology*, **4** (S1), 113–119.
17. Wakelin J. (1988). The role of serotonin in depression and suicide. *Advances in Biological Psychiatry*, **17**, 70–83.
18. Leckman J.F., Weissman M.M., Merikangas K.R., Pauls D.L. and Prusoff B.A. (1983). Panic disorder and major depression. *Archives of General Psychiatry*, **40**, 1060–1065.
19. Sheehan D.V., Coleman J.H. and Greenblatt D.J. (1984). Some biochemical correlates of panic attacks with agoraphobia and their response to a new treatment. *Journal of Clinical Psychopharmacology*, **4**, 66–75.
20. Ballenger J.C., Burrows G.D., Dupont R.L., Lesser I.M., Noyes R., Pecknold J.C., Rifkin A. and Swinson R.P. (1988). Alprazolam in panic disorder and agoraphobia. *Archives of General Psychiatry*, **45**, 413–422.
21. Breier A., Charney D.S. and Nelson J.C. (1984). Seizures induced by abrupt discontinuation of alprazolam. *American Journal of Psychiatry*, **141**, 1606–1607.
22. Fyer A.J., Liebowitz M.R,, Gorman J.M., Campeas R., Levin A., Davies S.O., Goetz D. and Klein D.F. (1987). Discontinuation of alprazolam tretment in panic patients. *American Journal of Psychiatry*, **143**, 303–308.
23. Priest R.G. and Montgomery S.A. (1988). Benzodiazepines and dependence. *Royal College of Psychiatry Bulletin*, **12**, 107–109.
24. Committee on Review of Medicines (1980). Systematic review of the benzodiazepines. *British Medical Journal*, **280**, 910–912.
25. Rickels K., Weisman K., Norstad N., Singer M., Stolz D., Brown A. and Danton J. (1982). Buspirone and diazepam in anxiety: a controlled study. *Journal of Clinical Psychiatry*, **43**, 81–86.
26. Marks I.M. (1983). Are there anti-compulsive or anti-phobic drugs? Review of the evidence. *British Journal of Psychiatry*, **140**, 338–347.
27. Telch M.J., Agras W., Taylor L.B., Roth W.T. and Galten C.C. (1985). Combined pharmacological and behavioural treatment for agoraphobia. *Behavioural Research Theory*, **23**, 325–333.

8

Benzodiazepines

INTRODUCTION

When benzodiazepines were first introduced in 1960 they were thought to be a safe and effective treatment for a wide range of anxiety related disorders. They proved to be a treatment which was particularly acceptable to patients because of the rapid relief of symptoms they experienced, relief which was not marred by accompanying unpleasant side effects. There seemed to be no reason why benzodiazepines should not be widely prescribed since they were considered to be lacking in dangerous side effects, safe in overdosage, and safer than the alternatives such as alcohol, etc., to which patients might otherwise turn for their anxiolytic effect. Benzodiazepines provided the practitioner with a safe and acceptable treatment to offer to the substantial proportion of patients in any practice whose complaint consisted of minor anxiety symptoms.

With so little restraint on prescribing it is not surprising that this class of drugs rapidly became very widely used. There was a steady increase in prescriptions in the UK for tranquillisers, hypnotics and sedatives during the 1960s and 70s though the rate of prescribing has dropped somewhat since then.[1] From a study carried out in general practice it appeared that diazepam was the most widely prescribed drug.[2]

The rapid spread in the use of benzodiazepines during the 1970s might not in itself be of particular concern to health workers: it is a source of satisfaction if a treatment which is both effective and safe is used to treat patients appropriately. What rang the alarm bells was the number of patients who continued to be prescribed benzodiazepines over very long periods. A survey of the use of anti-anxiety drugs carried out in the general community in the USA found that 1.6% of the population had been using these agents for a year or more.[3] Similar high levels of use were subsequently found in Europe

75

and an even higher level in the UK (3.1%).[4] The apparent national differences in the use of benzodiazepines are not stable and the rate of use in European countries other than the UK seems to have been rising in recent years. As it became apparent that some patients continued to take benzodiazepines over long periods of time, doubts began to be expressed about the proper role of benzodiazepines especially as convincing evidence of efficacy in the long term had not been properly established.

EFFICACY OF BENZODIAZEPINES

The standards applied for the demonstration of efficacy of the benzodiazepines were certainly somewhat less stringent than is expected nowadays when a new drug is introduced. Rather little attention was paid to identifying the patients for whom this form of treatment was most appropriate. Evidence of efficacy in mild anxiety was never required or obtained and the general attitude was that since the drugs were thought to be completely safe any possible relief they might provide to mildly anxious individuals would be welcome.

The possibility that the anxiety symptoms, particularly if they are mild, would resolve without intervention with drugs should not be overlooked. In some patients treatment with a benzodiazepine may be no more beneficial than brief counselling as was shown in a study of general practice patients in Oxford.[5] Furthermore, most studies have reported a high placebo response rate which suggests that spontaneous remission can be expected in a substantial number of patients.

LONG-TERM EFFICACY AND SAFETY

If a drug is only going to be used in short treatment courses the possible problems associated with long term usage are of secondary interest. It has however been quite obvious for a number of years that the benzodiazepines as a class are used by many people for long periods, and formal testing of long-term efficacy and safety should be carried out.

It seems that tolerance does not appear to develop early to the anti-anxiety effects of the benzodiazepines and they have been shown to be effective in reducing anxiety symptoms during continued use over several months.[6] Controlled studies which demonstrate the need for continued treatment are, however, sparse. We know a great deal about the natural history of depression in the absence of pharmacotherapy from the large body of studies which made double blind comparisons of antidepressant treatments against placebo. We know for example that 50% of patients suffering from depression who are treated with placebo following resolution of their symptoms will relapse in the next 6 months whether they have a history of previous episodes of depression or not. It has been possible to show the need for a lengthy period of maintenance treatment with antidepressants until the episode is resolved and to separate this type of treatment from the prophylactic treatment necessary for patients with recurrent depression. We do not have a comparable body of knowledge concerning the course of illness in patients with anxiety. It is clear that many patients continue to take benzodiazepines for longer than a year; what we need to know is what, if any, benefits are derived against which to offset the risks of long-term treatment.

The usual test of long-term efficacy is to treat with placebo a group of patients who have responded to an active treatment and compare their response during treatment with a similar group who continue with the active treatment. There is a specific problem in investigating benzodiazepines in this respect because rebound phenomena, often manifesting in an increase in anxiety, are seen to occur when the drug is withdrawn. None of the studies of longer-term treatment have satisfactorily overcome the problem of rebound anxiety.

In 1980 the Committee of Review of Medicines suggested that the absence of firmly based efficacy and safety data for the benzodiazepines from long-term studies should preclude their long-term use. They therefore recommended that benzodiazepines should not be used for more than 3 months[7] although this advice has apparently been largely ignored.

PROBLEMS WITH BENZODIAZEPINES

Withdrawal phenomena

If adequate long-term studies had been carried out it is possible that the risk of dependence with benzodiazepines might have been recognised earlier. As it was, the problem came to light through sporadic reports in the literature of cases of dependence developing, and by reports via post marketing surveillance systems. The size of the problem was not recognised at first and it was thought that the number of patients reported to have developed dependence was too small in relation to the total number of patients taking benzodiazepines to be of concern.

Dependence with benzodiazepines differs from some addictive drugs in that while patients actively seek a continuing supply of benzodiazepines from their family practitioner they do not as a rule increase their dosage markedly over time. The most important manifestation of the dependence is a withdrawal syndrome which may appear in as many as 44% of long term users when the benzodiazepine is reduced or withdrawn.[8]

Table 8.1.   Symptoms of withdrawal syndrome.

Symptoms easily mistaken for reappearance of original anxiety
  Increased tension
  Irritability
  Agitation
  Increased anxiety
  Disturbed sleep

Frequently occurring additional symptoms
  Perceptual distortions
  Vertigo
  Disorientation
  Depersonalisation
  Increased sensitivity to noise, light, pain, touch
  Disturbed gastrointestinal tract

Serious and less frequently occurring symptoms
  Fits
  Confusional states
  Frank depression
  Paranoid delusions

Serious symptoms such as fits and confusional states may occur although fortunately they are less frequent than the minor symptoms (Table 8.1). The withdrawal phenomena may be missed because some of the common symptoms are very similar to the original anxiety symptoms for which the benzodiazepine was prescribed. In about half the cases withdrawn from benzodiazepines there is an increase in anxiety, with irritability and sleep disturbance being prominent complaints. There may be increased tension accompanied by headaches and agitation and it is hardly surprising if such symptoms are assumed to be the resurgence of the original anxiety which had not fully resolved during benzodiazepine treatment.

The presence of unusual perceptual distortions such as apparent tilting movements of fixed objects, increased sensitivity to noise, light, pain and touch are thought to particularly characterise the severe withdrawal syndrome. A constellation of these symptoms is more likely to reflect a withdrawal syndrome than resurgence of the original anxiety. New symptoms about which the patient has not formerly complained are probably the most likely indicator of a withdrawal syndrome rather than anxiety. These increased symptoms would be expected to subside in a relatively short time while a resurgence in the original anxiety would not.

What contributes to the development of dependence?

An awareness of the factors which may contribute to the development of dependence can help in reducing the risk (see Table 8.2 and the sections which follow).

Dosage

In general it is thought that the use of higher doses increases the risk of dependence. This is not to say that low doses are without risk since dependence has been reported following treatment with very low doses of some benzodiazepines. If dosage plays a part it also seems likely that high potency benzodiazepines may have a greater risk of producing dependence than low potency compounds.

Particular benzodiazepines

There is a general belief that benzodiazepines with a short elimination half life have a greater potential for dependence, a view which has been encouraged by the finding that rebound phenomena are seen after very short treatments and withdrawal problems appear to be rather severe.[9,10] There are however few direct comparisons between different compounds which might confirm this possibility. Severe problems on withdrawal have not been reported with all benzodiazepines with a relatively short half life, for example temazepam, and it seems more likely that increased dependence potential is specific to particular compounds rather than related to pharmacokinetic factors.

Clinical impression suggests that more severe withdrawal problems are experienced with triazolam than some other benzodiazepines although there are no direct controlled comparisons. Some investigators have suggested there may also be greater difficulty during withdrawal from lorazepam and there is some support for this impression in a direct comparison of diazepam and lorazepam withdrawals.[9] Even the newer benzodiazepines such as alprazolam, introduced since the possible problem of dependence with this class of drugs was recognised, are not free of dependence potential, as was shown in the difficulty experienced by the majority of patients in a study of the gradual reduction of alprazolam after 3–6 months treatment.[11]

Length and continuity of treatment

Some patients who have been taking benzodiazepines continuously over a very long period will experience greater problems in withdrawing than those who have been treated for very short periods. This was shown in a study of withdrawal from benzodiazepines which found that problems are more likely with treatments that had continued for 5 months than those which had lasted only 6 weeks.[6] A definitive cut off point for length of treatment with any benzodiazepine to be sure of avoiding dependence has not been shown but is likely to be very short indeed.

Rebound effects have been reported after very short courses of treatment with benzodiazepines for anxiety. Withdrawal of the benzodiazepine after only 3 weeks in one study and 6 weeks in another[12,13] was accompanied by rebound increased anxiety.

Management of withdrawal

The real risk of the development of dependence on benzodiazepines in a substantial proportion of patients has been recognised in the medical profession for some years but has become a matter of concern to the public much more recently. Everybody agrees that benzodiazepines have been prescribed too freely and on too wide a scale. There is pressure to discontinue long term prescription of benzodiazepines both from the public and the medical profession and it is hoped these practical guidelines on the management of withdrawal will be helpful in what must be a cooperative effort.

Table 8.2.   Factors involved with withdrawal syndrome.

---

1. Sudden withdrawal
The withdrawal syndrome is more acute if benzodiazepines are withdrawn abruptly.

2. Dosage
Withdrawal problems are seen with both low and high dosage of benzodiazepines. Increased incidence with high dosage.

3. Particular drugs?
Short half life—there is some suggestion that withdrawal problem is more likely. However evidence that whole class of drugs is implicated is stronger than evidence against individual drugs.
Individual drugs—clinical impression suggests that withdrawal problem may be more likely with high potency drugs used at unnecessarily high dosage, e.g. triazolam, alprazolam, lorazepam.

4. Long uninterrupted treatment
Withdrawal problems are most likely if treatment has been prolonged and continuous. Problems are least likely if treatment has been for short period—less than 1 month, and intermittent.

Avoid dependence developing

Clearly the best way of avoiding dependence is to avoid unnecessary prescribing. Many patients prescribed benzodiazepines are suffering from depression and a greater awareness that the presence of anxiety symptoms may reflect an underlying depressive illness will lead to better treatment. It is difficult to detect those patients who are more likely to become dependent but treatments other than benzodiazepines should be preferred for those with a previous history of drug or alcohol dependence, and patients with personality disorders or long-standing neurotic symptoms. Brief counselling and a wait and see attitude will help reduce their use in mild anxiety or as hypnotics in minor sleep disturbance.

Gradual reduction

The severity of the problems encountered on withdrawing from benzodiazepines is undoubtedly increased if the drugs are stopped suddenly. It is on abrupt cessation that the more serious symptoms such as epileptic fits may been seen. Although some people seem able to withdraw abruptly, a programme of gradual reduction is wiser to reduce the risk of serious withdrawal effects.

The withdrawal symptoms may occur very rapidly if a short-acting benzodiazepine is being withdrawn but usually they emerge 4–5 days after the last dosage reduction and a weekly reduction programme is therefore recommended. A flexible programme which takes account of the severity of the symptoms will stand a better chance of success. The length of the reduction programme will probably depend on the individual and their motivation. No definite length can be recommended and periods varying in length from 1 month to 4 months have all been suggested.

In the latter stages of the programme it can be helpful to move towards drug holidays with intermittent dosage. The patient might take the drug on every alternate day, and if this is successful the dose could be given every third day and so on until the patient has confidence in the ability to remain medication free.

Concomitant medication

The effects of the withdrawal may be better tolerated with the help of other medication. An antidepressant instituted 1 month before the reduction programme begins and continued for some weeks after the programme has been found helpful. A low dose of β-blocking drugs, for example propranolol 40 mg twice daily, may help patients who have particular difficulty in tolerating withdrawal symptoms.

Reassurance and support

The success of the whole programme may well depend on the amount of social support and reassurance that can be provided and the assistance of friends and family should if possible be enlisted. Regular contact is needed preferably at weekly intervals to support the patient in coping with unwanted symptoms and to monitor the possible appearance of overt depression or even of undesirable coping mechanisms such as reliance on alcohol to alleviate symptoms. This will also provide the opportunity to help the patient master other techniques for coping with anxiety. Withdrawal from benzodiazepines in dependent patients is unlikely to be achieved overnight and even when a programme appears to have been successful the next 6 months or so must be regarded as a vulnerable period. Patients are most likely to go back on their resolve during this period and good clinical practice requires that continued observation and support will be provided.

HOW TO USE BENZODIAZEPINES

The ability of the benzodiazepines to bring about very rapid relief of symptoms of anxiety is valuable and it would be a pity if this real advantage were obscured by the current concern over their inappropriate long term use. A reminder of their best uses therefore seems timely (Table 8.3).

Benzodiazepines are very effective in reducing severe short-term anxiety and afford relief in only a few days. They will be most useful therefore in treating severe, disabling anxiety that is nevertheless expected to remit in a short time, for example an acute reaction to stress which is expected to resolve spontaneously within a week or two.

If benzodiazepines are to be used for alleviating anxiety symptoms they are best reserved for short-term treatment where the anxiety is so severe it is disabling to the patient. Even in such cases the length of treatment should be limited and the Royal College of Psychiatrists has suggested that a maximum period should be 1 month.[14]

Table 8.3.   Careful use of benzodiazepines.

- Use in severe cases of anxiety rather than mild
- Avoid in long-term illnesses
- Use lowest effective dose for the shortest period
- Use intermittent dosage
- Withdraw slowly

High doses of benzodiazepines are very effective in controlling panic but at the price of later increased dependence so that the lowest dose should be used. Panic disorder is better treated in the long term by antidepressants. Benzodiazepines are useful in the initial control over a 2–3 week period but should then be withdrawn.

To get the best out of benzodiazepines there are a few simple rules to follow the most important of which is probably to *start the way you mean to continue.*

1. First and foremost, establish the diagnosis and decide if benzodiazepines are the most suitable treatment. Anxiety symptoms may often mask

underlying depressive illness which would be better treated with an antidepressant.

2. In depression or mixed anxiety/depression or panic only use benzodiazepines for a short period and only as an adjunct to antidepressants.

3. Use benzodiazepines only in severe or incapacitating anxiety or sleep disturbance. If symptoms are mild avoid benzodiazepines.

4. Avoid benzodiazepines in chronic conditions such as long-standing anxiety states, obsessional states or personality disorders. Do not use for more than 4 weeks.

5. Before starting treatment with benzodiazepines enlist the cooperation of the patient. Advising about the risk of dependence will help the patient adhere to measures aimed at reducing the risk.

6. Avoid doses of benzodiazepines which are associated with the complete abolition of anxiety symptoms. A certain degree of anxiety is a normal experience in daily living and to accustom patients to its absence may be to their disadvantage in the long term.

7. Prescribe benzodiazepines in the way least likely to produce dependence: a strictly limited treatment period with the lowest possible dose (this may mean giving a lower dose than is provided by the manufacturer's formulation); encourage drug holidays for one to two days every three or four days particularly in prescribing for sleep disturbance.

8. When discontinuing benzodiazepines taper dose slowly downwards rather than ceasing treatment abruptly.

REFERENCES

1. Marks J. (1980). The benzodiazepines: use and abuse. *Arzneimittel Forschung*, **30**, 398–390.
2. Skegg D.G.G., Doll R. and Perry J. (1977). Use of medicines in general practice. *British Medical Journal*, **1**, 1561–1563.
3. Mellinger G.D. and Balter M.B. (1981). Prevalence and patterns of use of psychotherapeutic drugs: results from a 1979 national survey of American adults. In: *Epidemiological Import of Psychotropic Drugs* (Ed. G. Tognoni, C.Bellantuono and M. Lader), Elsevier, New York, pp. 117–135.
4. Balter M.B., Manheimer D.I., Mellinger G.D. and Uhlenhuth E.H. (1984). A cross-national comparison of antianxiety/sedative drug use. *Current Medical Research Opinion*, **8** (Suppl. 4), 5–20.
5. Catalan J., Gath D., Edmonds G. and Ennis J. (1984). The effects of non-prescribing of anxiolytics in general practice: controlled evaluation of psychiatric and social outcome. *British Journal of Psychiatry*, **144**, 593–602.
6. Rickels K., Case W.G., Downing R.W. and Winokur A. (1982). Long-term diazepam therapy and clinical outcome. *Journal of the American Medical Association*, **250**, 767–771.
7. Committee on the Review of Medicines (1980). Systematic review of benzodiazepines. *British Medical Journal*, **280**, 910–912.

8. Tyrer P., Owen R. and Dawling S. (1983). Gradual withdrawal of diazepam after long-term therapy. *Lancet*, **i**, 1402.
9. Tyrer P., Rutherford D. and Huggett T. (1981). Benzodiazepine withdrawal symptoms and propanolol. *Lancet*, **i**, 520.
10. Morgan K. and Oswald I. (1982). Anxiety caused by a short-life hypnotic. *British Medical Journal*, **284**, 942.
11. Fyer A.J., Liebowitz M.R., Gorman J.M., Campeas R., Levin A., Davies, S.O., Goetz D. and Klein D.F. (1987). Discontinuation of alprazolam treatment in panic patients. *American Journal of Psychiatry*, **144**, 303–308.
12. Pecknold J.C., McClure D.J., Fluin D. and Chang H. (1982) Benzodiazepine withdrawal effects. *Progress in Neuropsychopharmacology and Biological Psychiatry*, **6**, 517–522.
13. Power K.G., Jerrom D.W.A., Simpson R.J. and Michelle M. (1985) Controlled study of withdrawal symptoms and rebound anxiety after six week course of diazepam for generalised anxiety. *British Medical Journal*, **290**, 1246–1248.
14. Priest R.G. and Montgomery S.A. (1988). Benzodiazepines and dependence. *Royal College of Psychiatrists Bulletin*, **12**, 107–109.

9

Obsessive Compulsive Disorder

Obsessive compulsive disorder (OCD) has conventionally been classified with the anxiety states, for example in the DSM IIIR diagnostic system. There is, however, good reason to consider it as a separate condition. There are a number of features of OCD that differentiate it from the anxiety disorders including its later age of onset, equal prevalence in men and women rather than the two to one preponderance of women seen in anxiety or depression, and low level of placebo response. The major impetus for approaching OCD as a separate illness has however come from the observation that there is a differential response in OCD to a specific class of pharmacological treatments.

Recent epidemiological studies suggest that the incidence in the general population is higher than was generally thought. In the Epidemiological Catchment Area (ECA) study carried out in the United States, for example, 2.5% of the sample had a life-time risk and 1.5% had the condition in a 6 month period.[1] This figure may well be an underestimate because of the diagnostic criteria used in the study which make it likely that some patients with OCD would be included under other categories such as hypochondriasis or anxiety states. Those who suffer from OCD have a chronic condition with periodic exacerbations so that the illness represents a great deal of morbidity.

OCD tends to have two rather distinct presentations: those sufferers who are principally obsessional thinkers or ruminators and those who are principally ritualisers. In both groups the median age of onset is the same at around 24. In the ECA study the obsessional thinkers were found to be slightly commoner but there is a substantial overlap and both are regarded merely as different presentations of the same illness.

The condition is characterised by persistent thoughts or impulses which are acknowledged to be silly but recur despite resistance. After some time, resistance tends to wane since the thoughts or rituals recur anyway and resistance is mostly accompanied by a marked increase in anxiety. These obsessional thoughts and rituals are time-consuming and interfere with social relationships or jobs. The distress to the individual is often intense and the thoughts and rituals can be so demanding that their close family members are obliged to participate in the behaviour to assist them. The sufferers usually have obsessional traits of inflexibility, perfectionism and indecisiveness which predate the full blown obsessive compulsive condition.

OBSESSIONAL PERSONALITY VERSUS OCD

The distinction between those with an obsessional personality and the full obsessive compulsive disorder may sometimes be difficult and is, to some extent, arbitrary. The relationship between OCD and its related obsessional personality disorder is rather close and there is some indication that the obsessional personality disorder may be affected by pharmacological treatment which suggests that the two conditions are not separate. A full unravelling of these interrelationships awaits proper studies, however. For the practical purpose of treatment, the separation of the personality from the illness will depend on the strength of the obsessional thoughts and rituals which are surprisingly time-consuming and entrenched and the degree of functional disability they cause.

IDENTIFYING THE OBSESSIVE COMPULSIVE INDIVIDUAL

The recognition of the obsessional patient with rituals is easy, but patients with obsessional thoughts pose more of a problem. This is unfortunate since patients with obsessional ruminations appear to be more common than those with rituals and patients with rituals almost invariably have obsessional thinking as well.

Rituals related to dirt and a need for cleansing are sometimes obvious, for example marks between the fingers will identify overzealous handwashing. Rituals which concern security where patients endlessly check and recheck electricity points, gas taps, or locks, are also common. A simple question about checking habits is usually sufficient to pick these up but counting or touching rituals which oblige the person to perform an action or touch an object a certain number of times may be missed.

Identifying obsessional thoughts sometimes takes more time and skill. The commonest obsessional thoughts are disproportionate fears of contamination or worries about infection with illnesses that are often quite improbable. Worrying about catching AIDS from touching someone is a fairly recent addition to the content of obsessional thoughts and many obsessionals are currently being identified in AIDS clinics where they present with repeated requests for testing for HIV virus despite the unlikelihood of infection. It is not uncommon for obsessional patients to have unrealistic and disturbing thoughts of disaster: of killing or having killed. Some will avoid touching knives because of what they might do even though they recognise these thoughts as senseless. Endlessly indecisive and full of doubt they may reflect for hours on presumed misdeeds which sometimes happened many years ago.

OCD has indeed been described as the illness of doubt and many of the rituals and ruminations can be seen as the expression of the patient's inability to be sure. To cope with the lack of certainty obsessional patients are often meticulous in the extreme and will make lists of everything lest something be overlooked. When a patient arrives in the clinic with the remark that they have brought their list of questions the practitioner should be alerted to the need to consider OCD.

Obsessional preoccupations are time-consuming, unpleasant and cause the individual marked distress. They lead to deterioration of social relations or the ability to work. It is often only the close family who know about the doubts and obsessional thoughts and it is frequently the family that makes the sufferer consult the doctor. Although greatly distressed by the thoughts the obsessional patient believes that nothing can be done and they and their families sometimes suffer for years before reaching treatment.

HYPOCHONDRIACAL OBSESSIONS

Obsessional ruminations tend to be rather underdiagnosed and as a consequence poorly treated. The obsessional patient may make contact with the doctor because a preoccupation with contamination has spread to a fear of illness and reassurance is sought. The hypochondriacal fears which are integral to the illness sometimes lead such patients to become frequent attenders with 'fat files' before the real source of their problems is uncovered. Most practices have a number of patients who are tacitly considered to be hypochondriacs but who may well be suffering from the ruminative kind of OCD which will respond to appropriate treatment.

OCD AND DEPRESSION

Many patients with OCD suffer from concomitant depression and may develop quite profound depressive symptomatology. It has in the past been traditional to treat these depressive symptoms separately but more recent evidence points quite clearly to these depressive symptoms as being integral to the OCD. Separate treatment with standard tricyclic antidepressants is remarkably ineffective.

Early studies of clomipramine suggested that this drug had a specific advantage over the other tricyclic antidepressants in treating obsessional symptoms associated with major depression. This finding was followed by a series of studies that consistently demonstrated the superiority of clomipramine over placebo in the treatment of OCD.[2–9] These results were considered controversial at first and attempts were made to explain the efficacy of clomipramine in alleviating OCD as resulting simply from its antidepressant properties. However a pivotal placebo-controlled study found an independent anti-obsessional effect of clomipramine, which was effective in treating obsessive compulsive disorder, particularly obsessional thoughts, in patients who did not have concomitant depression.[2] Since then this efficacy in the treatment of OCD independently of an effect on depression has been confirmed in two very large multicentre studies that excluded concomitant depression.[9] It has become clear that clomipramine has a specific role in OCD with or without concomitant depression.

The consistent efficacy of clomipramine in treatment studies of OCD contrasts with the poor results seen with other conventional tricyclic antidepressants. Clomipramine has been compared with nortriptyline, amitriptyline, imipramine, desipramine, and with the monoamine oxidase inhibitor, clorgyline, and these comparators were either ineffective or significantly less effective.[5,10–14] The studies were by and large quite small so that it was quite surprising that significant differences could be demonstrated. The comparator antidepressant may have had some effect on depressive symptoms or obsessional symptoms in a few of the studies but any effect appears to be consistently less than with clomipramine. The consistent advantage reported with clomipramine suggested that the finding was very robust and it is no surprise that large multicentre studies are now confirming the early results.

One of the findings of clinical importance in the studies of the pharmacological treatment of OCD is that response to placebo is almost absent whether patients were suffering from concomitant depression or not. For example in our early 1980 study the placebo response was 5% compared with a 65% response for clomipramine. This is quite different from major depression where the placebo response rate is substantial and is another indication of the difference in the nature of the depressive symptoms in OCD and primary depression itself. The relatively poor response of depressive symptoms of OCD to conventional tricyclic antidepressants other than clomipramine also point to their being integral to OCD. Although more studies are still required to clarify the issue, the depressive symptoms of OCD appear to be part and parcel of the primary obsessional illness and should not be considered part of a separate disorder. The lack of response to placebo also provides a warning of the intractable nature of OCD if it is left untreated. OCD is a stable disorder running a chronic waxing and waning course in most cases.

IS OCD A SEROTONIN SPECIFIC DISORDER?

The relative specificity of action of clomipramine seen in the treatment studies is a fascinating issue. Why should clomipramine have a specific anti-obsessional effect whereas more traditional tricyclic antidepressants do not? One explanation is that the effect depends on the strong 5-HT uptake inhibiting properties of clomipramine. It is not possible to be sure because the active metabolite of clomipramine is noradrenergic, but when the relative lack of efficacy of antidepressants with less potent serotonergic effects is taken into account, the importance of clomipramine's 5-HT effects seems likely. It is as though the illness is unaffected by drugs acting on the noradrenaline or other neurotransmitter systems since other tricyclic antidepressants, benzodiazepines and neuroleptics are all found to be ineffective. Mianserin which has been found to be effective in OCD in one placebo controlled study has 5-HT_1, 5-HT_2 and 5-HT_3 antagonist effects.

The response of OCD to treatment with clomipramine appears to come about in a different way from the response of depression. In OCD the therapeutic response appears relatively rapidly and may be seen as early as after 1–2 weeks treatment.[15,9] In depression, on the other hand, a significant difference from placebo is not reliably seen until the fourth week of treatment. It is thought that the delay in response in depression is a function of the need for adaptive changes at 5-HT receptors in relation to the potentiation of 5-HT transmission brought about by clomipramine. The rapid response in OCD suggests that the adaptive changes are not needed in this illness and the therapeutic effect is brought about by some other means.

The importance of the 5-HT uptake inhibiting properties of clomipramine for its therapeutic effect has received support from the finding that other drugs with selective serotonergic effects are also effective. More recent studies have found that the selective 5-HT uptake inhibitor, fluvoxamine, is effective compared with placebo[16–18] and early studies on other 5-HT uptake inhibitors are promising. The strongest evidence to support the view that OCD is a serotonin specific disorder comes from the body of clinical treatment studies. The concept is however also supported by one report of a correlation between the lowering of 5-HIAA in the CSF and response to clomipramine,[19] which suggested an association between therapeutic response and central 5-HT activity. Neuroendocrine research in OCD has also provided reports that obsessional and anxiety symptoms are provoked by 1-m-chlorophenylpiperazine (mCPP), which has some 5-HT agonist effects,[20] and that metergoline, the 5-HT$_1$ and 5-HT$_2$ antagonist, reverses the anti-obsessional effect of clomipramine.[21]

Treatment with 5-HT uptake inhibitors

The pharmacological treatment of choice for OCD is a 5-HT uptake inhibitor. Clomipramine, the most thoroughly studied, is unfortunately the drug with the most side effects, and it is sometimes extremely difficult to persuade obsessional patients, preoccupied as they often are with worries about symptomatology, to tolerate the appropriate doses. In these cases it is important to begin with the lowest dose before raising it to the level the patient can tolerate. Response is seen in both the low 75 mg dose.[2] and the high doses.[9]

In view of the difficulties associated with treatment with clomipramine it seems more sensible to use one of the newer 5-HT uptake inhibitors which have fewer and less severe side effects than the TCAs. Unfortunately, these newer drugs have only been systematically investigated in relatively high doses which seemed effective. Again, to avoid the reaction of drug refusal because of side effects, it seems reasonable to begin at a low dose, rising slowly. Although a significant difference from placebo is reported in several studies at 2 weeks, response is not always rapid and most studies have found a slow general improvement over many weeks. The overall response rate is about 60% and residual obsessional symptoms usually remain. This level of response may sound disappointing but such gains are often associated with a dramatic improvement in the patient's social functioning and a return to normal life.

OCD AND TOURETTE'S SYNDROME

There is some evidence in a few cases for the co-occurrence of OCD and the tics and movement disorders which characterise Gilles de la Tourette's syndrome. In those with both OCD and Tourette's syndrome there is a disappointing response to 5-HT uptake inhibitors on their own. Tourette's syndrome is thought of as a dopamine disorder and responds to some extent to treatment with neuroleptics. The addition of neuroleptics to the 5-HT uptake inhibitors in the OCD patients with tics or movement disorders is thought to improve response but further studies are needed.

PSYCHOLOGICAL TREATMENTS IN OCD

Insight oriented treatments which aim to find the psychological origins of obsessional illness may lead to deterioration in OCD. Obsessional patients, understandably, have an obsessional propensity to ruminate excessively and searching for causes tends to increase the obsessional preoccupations. A more successful approach is to suppress the obsessional thoughts and rituals by behavioural treatments.

It is difficult to test the efficacy of behavioural treatments using adequate controls but there is evidence of improvement from small groups treated for short periods of 2–3 weeks with behaviour therapy, particularly in rituals in OCD treated with exposure.[4,8] In some cases, particularly when the patients are well motivated, these gains appear to be sustained for long periods although the studies which report this are open and flawed and do not take account of concomitant medication and other biases which make controlled studies mandatory. It appears that best results in the short term are seen with homework exposure treatments where the individual learns on their own to put up with the feared situation or contamination or to resist the rituals for gradually increased periods.

There are however doubts about the strength of these results. Those studies which used 5-HT uptake inhibitors or placebo as an adjunct to behaviour therapy have found a relative lack of efficacy in the placebo plus behaviour therapy treatment groups which suggests that 5-HT uptake inhibitors are more effective than behaviour therapy. Some investigators report a better response if 5-HT inhibitors are started before the behavioural treatments are initiated.

The treatment of choice in OCD, based on the existing results, would be 5-HT uptake inhibitors, but behavioural treatments may be used as an adjunct particularly for well-motivated ritualisers. There is little evidence of the efficacy of behaviour therapy in obsessional thinkers who form the majority of patients with OCD. In the presence of significant obsessional ruminations, which are rather difficult to approach with behavioural treatments, 5-HT uptake inhibitors are thought to be the only helpful treatment.

REFERENCES

1. Karno M., Golding J., Sorenson S.B and Burnam M.A. (1988). The epidemiology of obsessive compulsive disorder in five U.S. communities. *Archives of General Psychiatry*, **49**, 1094–1099.
2. Montgomery S.A. (1980). Clomipramine in obsessional neurosis, a placebo controlled trial. *Pharmaceutical Medicine*, **1**, 189–192.
3. Thoren, P., Asberg, M., Cronholm, B., Jornestedt L. and Traskman L. (1980). Clomipramine treatment of obsessive-compulsive disorder: I A controlled clinical trial. *Archives of General Psychiatry*, **37**, 1281–1285.
4. Marks, I.M., Stern, R.S., Mawson, D., Cobb J. and McDonald R. (1980). Clomipramine and exposure for obsessive-compulsive rituals. *British Journal of Psychiatry*, **136**, 1–25.

5. Insel T.R., Murphy D.L., Cohen R.M., Alterman I., Kilts C., and Linnoila M. (1983). Obsessive Compulsive Disorder—a double blind trial of clomipramine and clorgyline. *Archives of General Psychiatry*, **40**, 605–612.

6. Flament, M.F., Rapoport, J.L., Berg, C.J., Sceery, W., Kilts, C., Mellstram, B. and Linnoila, M. (1985). Clomipramine treatment of childhood obsessive compulsive disorder: a double-blind controlled study. *Archives of General Psychiatry*, **42**, 977–983.

7. Mavikassalian M., Turner S., Michelson L. and Jacob R. (1985). Tricyclic antidepressants in obsessive-compulsive disorder: antiobsessional or antidepressant agents? *American Journal of Psychiatry*, **142**, 572–576.

8. Marks, I.M., Lelliott, P., Basoglu M. and Noshirvani H. (1988). Clomipramine and exposure for compulsive rituals. *British Journal of Psychiatry*, **152**, 522–534.

9. de Veaugh Geiss J., Katz R. and Landau P. (1989). Treatment of obsessive compulsive disorder with clomipramine. *Psychiatric Annals*, **19**, 97–101.

10. Insel T.R., Mueller E.A., Alterman I., Linnoila M. and Murphy D.L. (1985). Obsessive compulsive disorder and serotonin: is there a connection? *Biological Psychiatry*, **20**, 1174–1188.

11. Leonard H., Swedo S., Rapoport J., Coffey M. and Cheslow D. (1988). Treatment of childhood obsessive compulsive disorder with clomipramine and desmethylimipramine: a double blind crossover comparison. *Psychopharmacology Bulletin*, **24**, 93–95.

12. Volavka J., Neziroglu F. and Yaryura-Tobias J.A. (1984). Clomipramine and imipramine in obsessive compulsive disorders. *Psychiatry Research*, **14**, 85–93.

13. Foa E.B., Steketee G., Kozak M.J. and Dugger D. (1987). Imipramine and placebo in the treatment of obsessive compulsives: their effect on depression and on obsessional symptoms. *Psychopharmacology Bulletin*, **23**, 8–11.

14. Ananth J., Pecknold J.C., van der Steen N. and Engelsmann F. (1980). Double blind comparative study of clomipramine and amitriptyline in obsessive neurosis. *Progress in Neuropsychopharmacology and Biological Psychiatry*, **5**, 257–264.

15. Montgomery S.A., Fineberg N. and Montgomery D. (1990). Early response in obsessive compulsive disorder with clomipramine: a placebo controlled study. *Progress in Neuropsychopharmacology and Biological Psychiatry*, in press.

16. Goodman W.K., Price L.H., Rasmussen S.A., Delgado P.L., Heninger G.R. and Charney, D.S. (1989). Efficacy of fluvoxamine in obsessive compulsive disorder, a double blind comparison with placebo. *Archives of General Psychiatry*, **46**, 36–43.

17. Perse T.L., Greist J., Jefferson J.W., Rosenfeld, R. and Dar, R. (1987). Fluvoxamine treatment of obsessive compulsive disorder. *American Journal of Psychiatry*, **144**, 1543–1548.

18. Cottraux J., Mollard E., Bouvard M., Marks I., Sluys M., Nury A.M., Douge R. and Ciadella P. (1990). Fluvoxamine and exposure in obsessive-compulsive disorders. *International Clinical Psychopharmacology*, **5**, 17–30.

19. Thoren P., Asberg M., Bertilsson L., Mellstrom B., Sjoqvist F. and Traskman L. (1980). Clomipramine treatment of obsessive compulsive disorder: Biochemical aspects. *Archives of General Psychiatry*, **37**, 1289–1295.

20. Zohar J., Insel T., Zohar-Kadouch R., Hill J.L. and Murphy D. (1988). Serotonergic responsivity in obsessive compulsive disorder. Effects of chronic clomipramine treatment. *Archives of General Psychiatry*, **45**, 167–172.

21. Benkelfat C., Murphy D., Zohar J. Hill J.L., Grover G. and Insel T.R. (1989). Clomipramine in OCD: further evidence for a serotonergic mechanism of action. *Archives of General Psychiatry*, **46**, 23–28.

10

Brief Depression

Much of the effort expended by research psychiatrists on the classification of depression has been directed towards defining the group of patients thought to respond best to conventional antidepressants. This approach has advantages clinically but it has some quite serious drawbacks, not least because it is likely to discourage the recognition of other depressive states and inhibit the investigation of newer, different treatments.

Major depression, which is diagnosed when the depressive symptoms have been present for 2 weeks or more, is seen in approximately 6% of the general population in one year. There is however a sizeable number of cases who complain of marked anxiety and depression which lasts only briefly, so briefly in fact that by the time they reach the clinic the symptoms may well have largely disappeared.

Primary care doctors have of course known for some time that these brief depressions are disruptive and swell the ranks of those patients labelled as frequent complainers. It has only recently been recognised, however, that this group of patients with brief depressions is as large as those with more persistent and conventional depression.

BRIEF EPISODES OF DEPRESSION AND SUICIDAL ACTS

Early indications that episodes of depression which last less than 2 weeks were important came from studies investigating the prevention of suicidal behaviour in individuals who had a history of repeated suicide attempts.[1-3] Although patients suffering from major depression were excluded from these studies, during the investigation very short depressive episodes were observed in the patients and these were associated with suicide attempts. Depressive symptoms lasting less than 2 weeks, registered on the Montgomery and

93

Asberg Depression Rating Scale (MADRS)[4] after 4 weeks in the study, predicted the occurrence of suicidal behaviour in patients treated with placebo subsequently during the 6 month study. It appeared that it was largely these intermittent episodes of depression, lasting less than 2 weeks, that were associated with suicidal behaviour. Subsequent studies of a similar group indicate that the suicide attempts appear to occur only during these short-lived episodes of depression.[5] The importance of these short-lived depressive mood states has been largely neglected. Now that they are recognised in the International Classification of Diseases (ICD 10). we may expect an increasing number of studies to help define their nature and identify effective treatments. The first series of studies succeeded in finding one effective treatment: low dose neuroleptics were found as early as 1979 to significantly reduce suicide attempts in these patients compared with placebo.

INCIDENCE OF BRIEF DEPRESSION

The relative prevalence of depression which has sufficient symptoms to satisfy DSM III criteria but does not last the 2 weeks expected of major depression has been recorded in follow-up studies of a normal population sample in Switzerland.[6] It was found that 10% of this population suffered from at least one episode of brief depression during a year and half of these, i.e. 5%, had recurrences with at least 12 episodes of brief depression during the year. Though not all of those identified had received medical care all had suffered from occupational or social impairment as a result of their condition. The group is therefore not only large numerically, it also represents substantial morbidity.

WHAT IS BRIEF DEPRESSION?

The recognition of the intermittent nature of brief depression is important for the management of a group of patients who take up a large part of the practitioner's workload. It is a very serious, disruptive illness associated with a high risk of suicidal behaviour. In spite of this it is an illness which is rather poorly recognised or treated. The cardinal features of the illness are its suddenness, severity, unpredictability, brevity, and recurrence. The severity and pattern of symptoms is very similar to major depression. Indeed during an episode patients would fulfil diagnostic criteria for major depression except that the duration of symptoms is less than 2 weeks. The episodes are short, mostly lasting 3 days, but disabling and as severe, while they last, as major depression. Both onset and remission are more sudden with these three day depressions but during the episode those afflicted are as socially and occupationally impaired as those with major depression.

These individuals have the great disadvantage of suffering from an illness which makes them tense, touchy, irritable and awkward in their relations with others and as a result they are sometimes characterised as personality disorders. Recent evidence, scarce though it is, does seem to suggest that the illness is early in onset and it probably predates the development of the characteristic difficulties in personal relations.[6] This implies that the adverse personality features are changes secondary to illness and that the concept of personality disorder is inappropriately applied. Some treatment studies have found that the personality disorder characteristics tend to lessen or disappear with improvement in their condition and this supports the notion of illness rather than life-long characterological disorder.

Some 8% of those with brief depressions in our series have occasional episodes which last longer than 2 weeks and in some the depression may last much longer. In these patients when the major depressive episode resolves the intermittent pattern of brief episodes reasserts itself. Though we lack definitive studies there is some indication that major depression superimposed on recurrent three day depressions may be less responsive to conventional antidepressants and these patients will need careful management particularly as the risk of suicide attempts is thought to be higher in these individuals with both conditions. It has even been suggested that certain psychotropic drugs, including tricyclic antidepressants, may precipitate longer lasting depression.

HOW CAN PATIENTS WITH THREE-DAY DEPRESSIONS BE RECOGNIZED?

Individuals with this condition appear to consult their doctors with the same sort of frequency as their more conventionally depressed counterparts and are apparently rather dissatisfied with the treatments offered. In my experience they form a fairly large proportion of those who bypass the primary care system and refer themselves to emergency hospital psychiatric services or casualty departments.

Severe symptoms and impairment of ability to work

The proportion of females to males is nearly two to one, similar to that reported with major depression although the difference between the sexes is less marked. These patients suffer from the range of depressive symptoms which would earn them the diagnosis of major depression if they persisted long enough. They complain of depression, irritability and anxiety with accompanying loss of energy, poor concentration, poor appetite and sleep loss. They also describe marked feelings of pessimism, common and urgent suicidal thoughts, and impulsiveness and seem more prone to attempt suicide than do those with more conventional depression. The ability to work is impaired not only because the episodes are severe but also because of the frequency of their recurrence.

Sudden onset

The suddenness of the onset and the severity of the depressive symptoms seem to be particularly disabling. The episodes usually occur unexpectedly out of the blue though they are sometimes associated with increased tension and lack of tolerance in the day or so before onset. Most sufferers say they have no idea that an episode has come until they wake up in the morning and discover that the awful thoughts have returned. Many of these individuals say that the power of the suicidal thoughts combined with impulsiveness and loss of the ability to tolerate things is particularly hard to bear.

Episodes not precipitated by events

The depressions are not reported to arise in response to precipitating adverse life events: life events are precipitated by the episode rather than vice versa. For example the hostility associated with the episode is reflected in increased emotional turmoil and conflict with close relatives. A vicious circle develops as the ability to cope with this type of stress diminishes which then increases the hostility and aggression. This produces a picture of a truculently awkward and obstructive depression which is particularly difficult to manage within the limits of the clinic. The unpredictable nature of the episodes contributes to the perception that these patients have unpredictable personalities.

Difficulties with relationships

The sudden change from apparently normal to depressed, with symptoms at least as severe as in major depression, is very difficult not only for the sufferer, but also for their close relatives, or for work colleagues to cope with. During the episodes the sufferers have a tense, explosive quality with a hostility to those around them which is almost palpable. At such times the family is perceived as intolerable rather than as a support and oversensitivity to criticism makes it difficult to tolerate the company of close relatives who notice and comment, often adversely, on the sudden mood shifts. Some of those who suffer from three day depressions learn to cope successfully with the illness on their own. They develop considerable knowledge of their condition and sometimes learn to retreat behind some kind of defence. Some, for example, disconnect the telephone for the duration; others, who can afford it, take two or three days away from work; yet others avoid relatives and friends and seek the neutral, non-intrusive company of strangers during the episodes. All report the difficulty during an episode of coping with emotional problems which they learn, if lucky, to put on hold until they recover.

Most of the individuals with brief depressions recognise the description of their illness immediately and with relief. For the most part they say they have rarely found a confidante who understands its nature and have therefore learned not to discuss it. It is therefore incumbent on the doctor to ask leading questions in deciding if this is the patient's problem. The question most easily recognised by sufferers is: *'Do you have episodes of depression which last only a few days but often recur a few weeks later?'*.

HOW TO TREAT BRIEF DEPRESSION

There have been few well controlled studies which makes it rather hard to give firm advice. Treatment with conventional antidepressants with their customary lag in response is unlikely to help a particular episode because the episodes are short-lived, though one might hope for a prophylactic effect in reducing the occurrence of episodes. At the moment we lack the formal studies to assess the efficacy of antidepressants; the single placebo controlled prophylactic study of low doses of mianserin reported some effect but not different to placebo.[3] If antidepressants are to be tried, the tricyclic antidepressants, amitriptyline, dothiepin, maprotiline and imipramine should be avoided since there is an increased risk of overdose in these patients, and these antidepressants are associated with a higher risk of death from overdose than others.

Neuroleptics in low doses

The treatment for which there is the most consistent evidence of a positive effect in this illness, drawn from placebo-controlled studies, is low dose neuroleptics. Treatment with 20 mg flupenthixol once a month produced significant reduction of suicidal behaviour compared with placebo in a severely at-risk group of repeated suicide attempters with brief depression.[1] The result is parallelled by a positive placebo-controlled study of another low dose neuroleptic, thiothixene, where improvement in borderline personality disorders was associated with a reduction of the features of impulsivity, affective instability and aggression.[7] Support for the usefulness of neuroleptics has recently come from a small placebo-controlled study of patients with borderline personality disorder in which trifluoperazine produced a significant reduction in 'suicidality' and anxiety.[8] Many clinicians agree that low dose neuroleptics are useful in patients labelled as having personality disorders and it seems that the concept of personality disorders with fixed unalterable traits may be misguided and simply reflects inappropriate treatment. The similar results reported in three placebo-controlled studies albeit in widely differing definitions of this group of patients is encouraging.

Lithium

There are reports that lithium, which is thought to work by its effects on the serotonin system, may be useful in this condition. It appears to reduce aggression in some handicapped patients and there are also reports of its being helpful in emotionally labile depressives.[9,10] It is possible that lithium could be helpful in reducing the aggression and impulsivity of the brief depression seen in the patients described in this chapter. There have also been some anecdotal reports of 5-HT uptake inhibitors being useful in this condition but there are as yet no controlled studies.

Monamine oxidase inhibitors

The conflicting data on MAOIs in conventional depression is contrasted with reports of the usefulness of these drugs in minor, intermittent depression or atypical depression. The same study which found trifluoperazine to be useful in borderline personality disorder also found tranylcypramine to be effective in reducing a range of depressive and anxiety symptoms including anger, impulsivity and suicidality.[8] It is difficult to be sure that these individuals suffered from brief depression, but it seems likely since they had rateable depression of less than 2 weeks duration. The affective instability seen in these patients which is one of the identifiers of borderline personality disorder in the DSM III diagnostic criteria matches brief depression rather closely. The possible superiority of MAOIs over conventional antidepressants in this group is suggested by the finding that phenelzine was superior to either placebo or imipramine in a mixed group of brief depression, defined according to Research Diagnostic Criteria[11] as intermittent depression of less than 2 weeks duration, and atypical depression.[12,13] The report of the usefulness of MAOIs in treating these patients who had rejection sensitivity and hysteroid dysphoria supports the notion that MAOIs may be helpful in brief depression. Prospective studies are however needed before MAOIs could be recommended with confidence for brief depressions.

Problems in treatment

Benzodiazepines and alcohol

The aggression, the impulsiveness, the acting out and the generally explosive nature of this group of patients makes it unwise to prescribe a drug which is associated with disinhibition. The use of benzodiazepines in this group is reported to be associated with increased violence and suicidal behaviour and they should therefore be avoided or used only with great caution. Alprazolam has been reported, for example, to increase suicidality and aggression.[14] Moreover the long-standing recurrent nature of the illness with the likely need for long-term treatment increases the chances of dependence developing. Alcohol tends to have a similar disinhibiting effect and is implicated in a high number of suicides and suicide attempts. Individuals with these intermittent brief episodes of depression often turn to alcohol or benzodiazepines for short-term relief with unfortunate consequences.

Psychotherapy

It is often thought that these patients become ill in reaction to precipitating stress and that psychotherapy would help with the problems with relationships. The evidence however suggests that the episodes are too frequent and unpredictable to be attributed to frictions in the family and at work. The handling of a positive psychotherapeutic relationship is a very difficult and demanding task in this group of patients and requires particular skills. Patients are prone to develop transference reactions which are particularly dangerous because of their suicidal tendencies. They do however seem to benefit when a neutral supportive role is adopted. Attempting to pursue psychotherapeutic insights is likely to increase emotions and increase the chances of suicide. These patients need support and kindness, preferably of an unthreatening, unemotional kind.

REFERENCES

1. Montgomery S., Montgomery D., McAuley R., Rani S.J., Roy D.H. and Shaw P.J. (1979). Maintenance therapy in repeat suicidal behaviour: a placebo controlled trial. In: *Proceedings 10th International Congress for Suicide Prevention and Crisis Intervention.* pp. 227–229.
2. Montgomery, S.A. and Montgomery D. (1982). Pharmacological prevention of suicidal behaviour. *Journal of Affective Disorders,* **4**, 291–298.
3. Montgomery S., Roy D. and Montgomery D.B. (1983). The prevention of recurrent suicidal acts. *British Journal of Clinical Pharmacology,* **15**, 183S–188S.
4. Montgomery S.A., Montgomery D., Baldwin D. and Green M. (1990). Intermittent three day depressions and suicidal behaviour. *Neuropsychobiology,* **147**.
5. Montgomery S.A. and Asberg M. (1979). A new depression scale designed to be sensitive to change. *British Journal of Psychiatry,* **134**, 382–389.
6. Angst, J. and Dobler-Mikola, A. (1985). The Zurich study—a prospective epidemiological study of depressive neurotic and psychosomatic syndromes IV Recurrent and nonrecurrent brief depression. *European Archives of Psychiatry and Neurological Sciences,* **234**, 408–416.

7. Goldberg S.C., Schulz S.C., Schulz, P.M., Resnick, R.J., Hamer, R.A. and Friedel R.O. (1986). Borderline and schizotypal personality disorders treated with low-dose thiothixene vs placebo. *Archives of General Psychiatry*, **43**, 680–686.
8. Cowdry R.W. and Gardner D.L. (1988). Pharmacotherapy of borderline personality disorder. *Archives of General Psychiatry*, **45**, 111–119.
9. Tyrer S.P., Walsh A., Edwards D.E., Berney T.P. and Stephens D.A. (1984). Factors associated with a good response to lithium in aggressive mentally handicapped subjects. *Progress in Neuropshycopharmacology and Biological Psychiatry*, **8**, 751–755.
10. Rifkin A., Quitkin F., Carrillo C., Blumberg A.G., Klein D.F. and Oaks G. (1972). Lithium carbonate in emotionally unstable character disorder. *Archives of General Psychiatry*, **27**, 519–523.
11. Spitzer R., Endicott J. and Robins E. (1975). *Research Diagnostic Criteria. Instrument No. 58*, New York State Psychiatric Institute, New York.
12. Liebowitz M.R., Quitkin F.M., Stewart J.W., McGrath P.J., Harrison W., Rabkin J., Tricamo F., Markowitz J.S. and Klein D.F. (1984). Phenelzine v imipramine in atypical depression: a preliminary report. *Archives of General Psychiatry*, **41**, 669–677.
13. Liebowitz M. R., Quitkin F.M. and Stewart J.W. (1988). Antidepressant specificity in atypical depression. *Archives of General Psychiatry*, **45**, 129–137.
14. Gardner D.L. and Cowdry R.W. (1985). Alprazolam-induced dyscontrol in borderline personality disorder. *American Journal of Psychiatry*, **141**, 98–100.

11

Suicide and Depression

Why do doctors remember so clearly their patients who have killed themselves? Doctors grow accustomed to death yet suicide continues to make an impact. The families and those close to those who kill themselves are also marked by the suicide. Knowledge of history of illness in the family is normally imprecise; many find it difficult to remember the phrase used about the illness of a distant relative except when it is suicide. Then the memory is sharp or the subject may be abruptly avoided no matter how long ago the death occurred. It is as though the relative is scarred by the experience, death from other causes does not seem to cause this reaction.

Suicide is relatively common: between three and four thousand deaths from suicide are recorded each year in England and Wales and the official figure is undoubtedly an underestimate. The verdict of suicide in the UK, for example, is legally determined and requires evidence of the person's intent to take their life; in cases where there is insufficient evidence an open verdict is recorded. In the official estimates of the suicide rate, based on Coroners' reports, only deaths that have been legally determined as suicide are included and no account is taken of the open verdicts, which are quite common, and many of which are likely to have been intentional but unproven suicides. Doubt also attaches to the verdicts of accidental death as some of those who take their lives by more violent means such as drowning or jumping may well be recorded as accidental death.

The requirement of evidence of intent may also bias the figures in underestimating the impulsive, ambivalent or disorganised suicide where little legal evidence of intent could be expected compared with the proportion of suicides who were persistently depressed, and more likely to leave evidence of their plans. A better measure of the suicide rate, which would take account of the open and accidental death verdicts, suggests that in the UK the actual rate is possibly some 30–40% higher than the official figures suggest.[1,2]

SUICIDE IN MAJOR DEPRESSION

A number of the core symptoms of depression are seen to predict suicide attempts in the vulnerable. In addition to the severity of depression, suicidal thoughts, poor sleep and pessimism about the future, in some studies tagged as hopelessness, seem to emerge as reliable predictors.[3,4] Some studies have suggested that impaired concentration and loss of interest, as well as social withdrawal, reflect a higher risk. The risk of suicide is reported to be high in the first week after assessment of a patient's depression. Indeed 42% of suicides were found in one study to have consulted their general practitioner or psychiatrist within a week of their death with half of these having made a clear-cut threat.[5]

The risk of death from suicide is substantially raised in depressive illness and a consistent figure of around 15% of depressives who eventually kill themselves is seen in the early surveys of cause of death[6-12] (Table 11.1). These estimates have been borne out in more recent follow-up studies of depressed patients[13] and in large scale prospective studies that have followed up general population samples for considerable numbers of years.[14,15] It does not seem to matter whether the depressions are characterised as endogenous or not but it does matter that the illness is recurrent.

Table 11.1. Suicide in depression.

	Study length	Deaths in study	% Suicides
Langeluddeck 1941[6]	40 years	268/341	15.3
Slater 1938[7]	30 years	59/138	15.3
Lundquist 1945[8]	20 years	119/319	14.3
Schulz 1949[9]	5 years	492/2004	13.4
Stensted 1952[10]	20 years	42/216	14.3

Studies which have tried to establish the mental state at the time of death, which is not easy, have reported varying rates of depression. Barraclough and Palin reported that more than 60% were depressed but lower rates, of 30–45%, are reported in other studies.[12,15,16] The lack of concordance in the estimates may well be due to the differing criteria used in the definition of depression. When these studies were carried out the diagnostic category of brief depression and its associated increased risk of suicidal behaviour had not been recognised. As brief depressions have not been separately identified in the studies the contribution to the suicide figures of individuals suffering from this condition cannot be properly assessed but it is likely that they account for some of the difference in the estimates of depression associated with suicide.

A substantial proportion of those who commit or attempt suicide are labelled as personality disorders. In the series of prospective studies on previous suicide attempters carried out in Edinburgh it was reported that of those who later completed suicide virtually none were considered to have a normal personality.[17] There appeared to be a closer relationship between suicide and major depression in older patients and personality problems in younger patients particularly males. The association of personality disorder with suicide was also reported in a large study which followed up 50 000 Swedish conscripts for 13 years.[18] Personality variables were the best predictors of suicide, namely poor emotional control, history of misconduct at school, contact with welfare or authorities, or few friends. These findings are supported in a prospective study of a group of adolescents who had made a suicide attempt where disorders of adjustment and emotional instability were reported to be conducive to suicide.[19]

There also appears to be a significant genetic component in suicide as both twin studies[20] and adoption studies[21] have shown and this appears to be independent of depression. The large Danish adoption study found that suicide occurred more frequently in the biological relatives of adopted depressives particularly where the illness was bipolar rather than unipolar or neurotic depression. Interestingly the highest incidence of suicide was seen in the biological relatives of those adoptees who had affective reactions appearing as sharp, brief depressive episodes in rather impulsive individuals.[22] There is an association between brief depressive episodes and increased risk of suicide attempts in those with personality problems[3] and those without[22] and the finding that this phenomenon may have a genetic component is important.

ATTEMPTED SUICIDE OR SUICIDAL BEHAVIOUR

These terms are used in overlapping ways, which makes sense since it is often difficult to be sure whether or not the individual wanted to die. Many unsuccessful suicides profess a degree of ambivalence to the outcome so that a definition based on intent is not helpful. The introduction of the neologisms pseudosuicide or parasuicide applied to all survivors of suicidal behaviour has had the unfortunate effect of downgrading the danger inherent in attempts, and of allowing highly dangerous suicidal behaviour to be dismissed as mere gestures. Survival depends on many chance factors: whether the individual vomits or not, whether an overdose is taken after meals thereby slowing the absorption of the drug, whether the liver is able to detoxify the drug, whether the individual is a fast or slow metaboliser, whether the heart is susceptible to damage. Many of us know of individuals who have died following very small overdoses just as there are survivors who have taken massive overdoses.

It is folly to ignore the risk of a so-called gesture or the long-term increased risk of repetition and death.

RECOGNITION OF THE HIGH RISK GROUP

There do appear to be differences between those who commit suicide and those who make unsuccessful attempts but it is not possible to predict with accuracy on an individual basis. The suicides are more often older and male whereas unsuccessful suicides are more often younger and female but such a broad separation is unlikely to be helpful in assessing the risk in a particular individual. The group at risk of a suicide attempt or of suicide is large and it is important to identify the broad high risk categories in order that appropriate particular care is taken with the management of these individuals.

Previous attempts predict suicide

Most follow-up studies have identified a previous attempt as the most clearly and clinically defined predictor of a subsequent suicide. Those who attempt suicide are about a hundred times more likely to die by suicide than the general population. In a comprehensive follow-up of 3265 people who had made a suicide attempt in Finland the highest risk of suicide was in the year or two following the suicide attempt and declined thereafter.[23] In this study the suicide rate of 2.6% over 2 years following a suicidal attempt increased to 3.6% in those with a history of a previous attempt and remained higher for the 7 year follow-up. The rate was three times higher in males than in females and of those who killed themselves about half had attempted previously. A history of a previous attempt can be readily verified by questioning and, since it is the most easily identified predictor of a future suicide attempt, should be noted on every case record as a reminder that caution is needed. Some 20% of those who make a suicide attempt make another in the subsequent year and the risk rises with a history of more than one attempt. As the chance of death from suicide appears highest in the year or two following an attempt, patients with a history of suicidal behaviour need to be treated as being at a very high risk during this period.

Brief depressions

Brief but frequently recurring depressive episodes have been found to predict suicide attempts .[3,4] In the studies of Montgomery et al.[24] two-thirds of these brief episodes of depression lasted between 2–4 days but recurred irregularly some 2–3 weeks later. The pattern of symptoms predicting suicide, apart from the severity of depression were suicidal thoughts, pessimism about the future, loss of appetite, loss of sleep and lassitude or tiredness. The unpredictability of the recurrence along with a very rapid onset is described as greatly increasing the unbearability of the condition. It seems likely that the rapidly evolving and resolving depression itself will be both a cause and a predictor of suicide attempts. In some individuals both major depression and brief depressions occur and the risk of suicide attempts is even greater.

Personality problems

There is some circularity in the finding that individuals labelled as having personality disorders contribute disproportionately to the numbers of those who make suicide attempts and also those who commit suicide, since suicidal behaviour is one of the features which goes towards making the personality disorder diagnosis. It is also possible that some of the features of personality disorder arise in individuals who have a recurrent pattern of brief depressions which are associated with suicidal behaviour. The features of personality disorder are nonetheless useful pointers in identifying patients who may be at a high risk of suicide. Several studies have shown that the presence of aggression predicts suicidal behaviour[25,26] as indeed does the diagnosis of sociopathy or personality disorder.[27] It is difficult to know from these reports whether the higher rate was found in individuals with personality problems who had brief depressions or in personality disorders without depressive episodes. Caution suggests however that the identification of these features should signal a higher risk.

Alcohol abuse

In the UK alcohol is implicated in a substantial proportion of deaths from overdose and the studies that have retrospectively examined diagnoses suggest that some 22% of suicides had been given the diagnosis of alcoholism.[28] The pattern of drinking which predicts suicide seems to change with age: in the younger group excessive bout drinking predicts suicide whereas in the older group long-term alcoholics are more at risk. It seems as though alcohol may act in two unfortunate ways. Alcohol is reported to induce depression and suicidal thoughts, particularly during withdrawal but at the same time to disinhibit the individual allowing the suicide attempt to be carried out. Alcohol is also used by many as inappropriate treatment for their depressions with unfortunate consequences. Alcohol is also used to wash down overdoses thereby potentiating the risk. Benzodiazepines are relatively safe in overdosage on their own but quite dangerous in combination with alcohol.

Social and demographic factors

General social and demographic variables have been studied by many investigators and there is general consistency in the finding that certain factors show a persistent but weak effect in predicting suicide, though this can only be seen in large studies. Suicide is more commonly seen in men than in women despite the finding that women attempt suicide more frequently than men. There appears to be a relationship with age, particularly with men, older men committing suicide more frequently than younger men. In women the risk of suicide is commoner between the ages of 50 and 60. Suicide is more common among the single, both men and women, than among the married though the difference is more marked among men. All the studies identify the importance of social isolation as a predictor of suicide whether measured in terms of living alone or the absence of social support. In this context the finding of a lower suicide rate in regular church goers is interesting. Recent isolation, as in the newly divorced or widowed, is also a predictor of suicide.

REDUCING THE SUICIDE RATE

People who kill themselves use the means available and as a result there are national differences in the favoured method. The ready access to firearms in countries like the USA is reflected in the suicide statistics in the increased use of this method relative to other countries. Men seem to prefer violent means such as hanging, shooting, jumping, and since these methods are more effective it is possible that the higher suicide rate in men is partly a product of their violence. In contrast, women, especially younger women, seem to prefer to overdose, a method which is less reliable.

On the face of it the most obvious way of reducing the suicide rate would be to restrict the easy access to firearms in the USA since the alternate means adopted may not be so easy or effective. The reduction in the domestic

Table 11.2. Domiciliary treatment of depression in the suicide risk patient.

1. Treat depression energetically. Use antidepressants in full doses.
2. Use only safer antidepressants. Avoid amitriptyline and dothiepin and other TCAs associated with toxicity in overdose.
3. Do not relax on response. Greatest danger on apparent recovery.
4. Continue treatment for at least 4 months after response.
5. If depression is recurrent use prophylaxis.

availability of lethal coal gas and replacement with natural gas was thought by some to be associated with a reduction of the suicide rate in the UK. Likewise, the reduced availability of barbiturates as sedatives, when they were replaced by benzodiazepines, has been thought to have an effect on the suicide rate, although the data are difficult to interpret. Benzodiazepines are associated with disinhibition and consequent provocation of suicidal behaviour and it is possible that the rise in suicide attempts in the 1970s could have been influenced by the increased use of these drugs.

Similar reasoning has suggested that a reduction in the availability or use of the older TCAs and the substitution of safer antidepressants might reduce the suicide rate in depression. A fatal outcome is very much more likely with the older TCAs than with the newer antidepressants[29,30] and, as a recent large-scale analysis of the outcome of overdose of amitriptyline or mianserin prescribed in general practice showed,[31] there is also considerably more use of hospital intensive care following overdose with amitriptyline. The use of safer antidepressants would be expected to reduce the morbidity and the mortality of suicide attempts.

The finding in a very large long-term efficacy study that maprotiline increases the suicide attempt rate compared with placebo despite efficacy in reducing the relapse rate of depression is disturbing.[32] The provocation of suicide attempts by maprotiline is consistent with earlier reports that it is associated with persistent suicidal thoughts compared with other safer antidepressants. The finding that an established antidepressant may provoke suicide attempts raises the possibility that other toxic antidepressants are unsafe because they too may provoke suicide attempts by similar but unknown mechanisms. Amitriptyline, for example, was seen to be associated with more suicide attempts than mianserin in the large general practice prescription event monitoring study which is independent of the increased toxicity reported.[31]

REDUCING THE RISK OF SUICIDE IN MAJOR DEPRESSION

Probably the most important issue is to recognise the major depression and treat it energetically using effective doses. It is an unfortunate fact that in prescribing an antidepressant the doctor may be providing the means which the patients may use to harm themselves. For this reason it is important to use the safer antidepressants available in the groups at special risk. Many suicides seem to occur after the individual has begun to make a recovery. This is attributed by some, without much data to back them up, to an improvement in retardation providing the impetus to self harm which had been lacking. Whatever the mechanism, the phenomenon is a clear warning that treatment of depression should continue for long enough to ensure the

Table 11.3. Supportive measures to reduce suicide risk in major depression.

1. Ensure the patient is not left alone. Mobilise friends and relatives to support on a rota. This support should be sympathetic but emotionally undemanding.
2. Medication should be in the hands of a reliable relative or friend.
3. The role of the doctor should be supportive firm and optimistic. Stress the sympathy with the depressed state but reassure that depression passes with effective treatment.
4. Express confidence that treatment will work in the end.
5. Explain that treatment takes a bit of time.
6. Explain the patient may feel worse initially while the medication gets to work.

episode is past, that is, for at least 4 months after response. Treatment should not be discontinued, as it often is, when response is first seen.

The suicides in major depression are mainly found in recurrent depression so that effective prophylaxis is essential whether in unipolar or bipolar disorders.

During the depressive episode it is important to encourage relatives and friends to provide a network of sympathetic and understanding support. The patient should be left alone as little as possible. It is safer to collect up all medication in the house, aspirin, paracetamol and the prescribed antidepressant treatments, and put them in the charge of a reliable relative or friend. The doctor can do much by being supportive and optimistic. It is particularly important to stress that the treatment will work even if this takes time.

In the case of a serious suicide risk remember that ECT is considered the most effective treatment for depression particularly where delusions or aggressive suicidal urges are present. Tables 11.2 and 11.3 give guidelines for reducing the risk of suicide in depressed patients.

REDUCING THE RISK OF SUICIDE IN BRIEF DEPRESSION

The risk of suicide and suicide attempts has only recently been recognised in brief depressions so that reasonable plans to reduce the risk of suicide and suicide attempts have not been thoroughly evaluated or adopted. The most important risk factors have been discussed but if any of the following are present the dangers are greatly increased and appropriate caution is needed.

● Previous attempt,
● Sociopathic traits or aggression,
● Concomitant alcohol or benzodiazepine dependence,
● Recent major depression.

Table 11.4. How to minimise the risk of suicide in brief depression.

Lifestyle advice
   1. Recognise the intermittent nature of illness
   2. Retreat emotionally and possibly physically during episodes
   3. Choose appropriate occupation:
   (a) with low emotional content, and
   (b) which will allow unpredictable days off
   4. Avoid family conflicts when ill, require that family be tolerant and non-intrusive

Drug treatment
   1. Treat over long not short term
   2. Use safe drugs preferentially
   (a) low dose neuroleptic e.g. flupenthixol
   (b) lithium
   (c) MAOIs
   3. Avoid toxic TCAs which may lead to suicide
   4. Avoid benzodiazepines or alcohol

It is helpful to discuss with the patient the exact nature of the illness in order that they may consider taking a few precautions. If they recognise that they have an intermittent disorder which lasts only a few days they may find it safer to steel themselves with some sort of emotional defence for a few days or to change their lifestyle to allow intermittent time off work. Some find it helpful to avoid close family members over the depressions because they find them to be intrusive and critical.

The drugs that are most likely to be effective in this condition are low dose neuroleptics and possibly MAOIs or lithium. The TCAs, particularly amitriptyline, dothiepin and maprotiline, should be avoided: there is little evidence that they help and clear evidence of dangers. Likewise benzodiazepines and alcohol need to be avoided (see Table 11.4).

REFERENCES

1. Ovenstone I.M.K. (1973). A psychiatric approach to the diagnosis of suicide and its effect upon the Edinburgh statistics. *British Journal of Psychiatry*, **123**, 15–21.
2. McCarthy P.D. and Walsh D. (1966). Suicide in Dublin. *British Medical Journal*, **1**, 1393–1396.
3. Montgomery S.A., Roy D., and Montgomery D.B. (1983). The prevention of recurrent suicidal acts. *British Journal of Clinical Pharmacology*, **15**, 183S–188S.
4. Montgomery S., Montgomery D., McAuley R., Rani S.J., Roy D.H. and Shaw P.J. (1979). Maintenance therapy in repeat suicidal behaviour: a placebo controlled trial. *Proceedings 10th International Congress for Suicide Prevention and Crisis Intervention*, pp. 227–229.
5. Barraclough B., Bunch J., Nelson B. and Sainsbury P. (1974). A hundred cases of suicide: clinical aspects. *British Journal of Psychiatry*, **125**, 355–373.

6. Langeluddeck A. (1941). Uber Lebenservartung und Rucksfallhaufigkeit bei Manisch-depressiven. *Psychiatr. Hyg.*, **13**, 1–14.
7. Slater E. (1938). Zur Erbpathologie des manisch-depressiven Irreseins: Die Eltern und Kindern von Manisch-depressiven. *S. Gesamte Neurol. Psychiatr.*, **163**, 1–47.
8. Lundquist G. (1945). Prognosis and course in manic-depressive psychoses. *Acta Psychiatrica Neurologica Scandinavica*, (Suppl. 35) 1–96.
9. Schulz B. (1949). Sterblichkeit endogen Geisteskranker und ihren Eltern. *S Menschl. Vererb Konstitutions Lehre*, **29**, 338–367.
10. Stensted A. (1952). A study in manic-depressive psychosis, clinical, social and genetic investigations. *Acta Psychiatrica Neurologica Scandinavica*, (Suppl. 79), 1–111.
11. Pitts F.N. and Winokur G. (1964). Affective disorder III Diagnostic correlates and incidence of suicide. *Journal of Nervous and Mental Disorders*, **139**, 176–181.
12. Robins E., Murphy G.E., Wilkinson R.H., Gassner S. and Kayes J. (1959). Some clinical considerations in the prevention of suicide based on a study of 134 successful suicides. *American Journal of Public Health*, **49**, 888–798.
13. Miles C.P. (1977). Conditions predisposing to suicide: a review. *Journal of Nervous and Mental Disorders*, **16**, 231–246.
14. Helgason T. (1964). The epidemiology of mental disorder in Iceland. *Acta Psychiatrica Scandinavica*, **40** (Suppl.), 173.
15. Barraclough B.M. and Pallin (1975). Depression followed by suicide: a comparison of depressed suicides with living depressives. *Psychological Medicine*, **5**, 55–61.
16. Dorpat T. and Ripley H.S. (1960). A study of suicide in the Seattle area. *Comprehensive Psychiatry*, **1**, 349–359.
17. Kreitman N. (1977). *Parasuicide*. Wiley, Chichester, p. 167.
18. Allebeck P., Allgulander C. and Fisher L.D. (1988). Predictors of completed suicide in a cohort of 50,456 young men: role of personality and deviant behaviour. *British Medical Journal*, **297**, 176–178.
19. Otto U. (1972). Suicidal acts by children and adolescents. *Acta Psychiatrica Scandinavica*, **233** (Suppl.), 1–123.
20. Kety S. (1986). Genetic factors in suicide. In: *Suicide* (Ed. A. Roy), Williams and Wilkins, Baltimore.
21. Schulsinger F., Kety S.S., Rosenthal D. and Wender P.H. (1979). A family study of suicide. In: *Origin, Prevention and Treatment of Affective Disorders* (Ed. M. Schou and E. Stromgren), Academic Press, New York.
22. Angst A. (1988). Presented at British Association of Psychopharmacology Annual Meeting Cambridge.
23. Lonnqvist J. (1987) Personal communication.
24. Montgomery S.A., Montgomery D.B., Baldwin D. and Green M. (1990). Intermittent 3 day depressions and suicidal behaviour. *International Neuropsychobiology*, in press.
25. Angst J. and Clayton P. (1986). Premorbid personality of depressive, bipolar and schizophrenic patients with special reference to suicidal issues. *Comprehensive Psychiatry*, **27**, 511–532.
26. West D.J. (1965). *Murder followed by Suicide*. Heinemann, London.
27. Shafi M., Carrigan S., Whittinghill J.R. and Derrick A. (1985). Psychological autopsy of completed suicide in children and adolescents. *American Journal of Psychiatry*, **142**, 1061–1064.
28. Robins E. (1986). Completed suicide. In: *Suicide* (Ed. A. Roy), Williams and Wilkins, Baltimore.

29. Montgomery S.A. and Pinder R.M. (1987). Do some antidepressants promote suicide? *Psychopharmacology*, **92**, 265–266.
30. Cassidy S. and Henry J. (1987). Fatal toxicity of antidepressant drugs in overdose. *British Medical Journal*, **295**, 1021–1024.
31. Inman W.H.W. (1988). Blood disorders and suicide in patients taking mianserin or amitriptyline. *Lancet*, **ii**, 90–92.
32. Rouillon F., Phillips R., Serrurier D., Ansart E. and Gerard M.J. (1989). Prophylactic efficacy of maprotiline on relapses of unipolar depression. *L'encephale*, **15**, 527–534.

12

Antidepressants in Overdose

THE SIZE OF THE PROBLEM

Antidepressants have made an impressive contribution to improving the quality of life of depressed patients but the uncomfortable fact remains that some of those treated will use antidepressants as a means of harming themselves. The problem of self poisoning is not a small one and has increased over the last 20–30 years to become a major public health issue. In England and Wales there are some 110 000 admissions to hospital each year from accidental or deliberate self poisoning and since this figure takes no account of the substantial proportion of overdoses who are not referred to hospital it almost certainly underestimates the total number of overdoses. Some 25% of overdose cases known to the general practitioner for example may not be referred to hospital[1] and other cases recover from an overdose without contacting either the general practitioner or hospital.

THE SERIOUSNESS OF THE PROBLEM

There is a commonly held view that many patients who take overdoses, particularly those who make repeated attempts, are making threats or gestures and are not seriously at risk. It is however a mistake to underestimate the morbidity of the group of patients who have episodes of deliberate self harm since some 20% may be expected to repeat their suicidal behaviour within a year and 1–3% of those with an admission to hospital for self harm commit suicide within the next year.[2]

Depression is associated with excessive mortality[3-5] and suicide and accidental death account for an excess proportion of all deaths. The risk of death from suicide in patients treated for depression has been estimated at

30 times that of the general population.[3] Much depression is missed in primary care and in one study of a series of 44 depressed patients admitted to a centre for self poisoning, less than one-third were receiving antidepressants.[6] More than half of these patients were receiving benzodiazepines which is worrying both because it represents the difficulty in identifying those at risk of suicide and because benzodiazepines are known to lead to an increase of suicidal attempts through their disinhibiting effect.[7,8]

The clinician faces a dilemma in treating depression because it is only too well known that many of the antidepressant treatments available are dangerous in overdose. There are certain known risk factors which increase the likelihood of an overdose but it remains difficult to predict which individual patients will make a suicide attempt. Appropriate caution in the management of depressed patients in high risk groups may help reduce the risk of overdose, but the high level of toxicity of some widely prescribed antidepressants is disturbing. Improved safety in overdose of antidepressants is therefore an important consideration in choosing which antidepressant to prescribe.

RELATIVE TOXICITY OF ANTIDEPRESSANTS IN OVERDOSE

Hospital admissions

Some measure of the relative toxicity of different antidepressants in overdose can be derived from statistics of hospital admissions. A survey of published studies reported by Frommer and colleagues in 1987 which included 2536 patients showed that over 50% of TCA overdoses were associated with significant cardiac complications.[9] An analysis by the National Poisons Centre[10] of a group of patients who had taken an overdose of maprotiline, which also has a modified tricyclic structure, showed that 29.3% were admitted in coma, and 20% had convulsions, a finding also reported in other surveys.[11] The high incidence of serious sequelae in TCA overdose is in contrast to the lack of toxic effects with the second generation antidepressants such as mianserin.[12]

A better register of the relative toxicity of antidepressants in overdose is of course the mortality rate. The percentage of patients who died following TCA overdose in the Poisons Centre series was 3.3 and a later survey reported a death rate of 2.2%.[9] Figures taken from hospital admissions are to some extent misleading since the largest proportion of deaths occur outside the hospital.[10] A better measure both of the size of the problem and of the relative toxicity of different antidepressants may be obtained from an analysis of national mortality statistics.

National mortality statistics

Toxicity of older TCAs

In England and Wales fatal poisonings are reported at Coroners' inquests and the mortality statistics are published by the Office of Population and Censuses. The most direct measure of toxicity of an antidepressant in overdose is provided where the cause of death is attributed to a single drug rather than to many different drugs. An index of toxicity can be derived by relating the number of fatal overdoses reported to the use of an antidepressant calculated as the ratio of total fatalities to prescriptions or as the ratio of fatalities to patients treated.

One recent analysis of overdose with widely used antidepressants calculated the number of patients treated from the amount of drugs sold using defined daily doses and durations of treatment.[13] The figures were based on Office of Population and Census data and International Market Service market statistics for England and Wales for the period 1977–84. There was a wide variation in fatal poisonings with different antidepressants and certain antidepressants had notably greater toxicity than others (Table 12.1). Amitriptyline and dothiepin appear to be the most dangerous in overdose when compared with other antidepressants.

Table 12.1. Incidence of fatal overdose with antidepressants in UK.

Drug	Fatal overdose per million prescriptions 1975–84[a]	Fatal overdose per million patients 1977–84[b]
Dothiepin	50	143
Amitriptyline	46.5	166
Maprotiline	37.6	103
Doxepin	31.3	106
Imipramine	28.4	106
Trimipramine	27.6	87
Clomipramine	11.1	32
Mianserin	5.6	13

[a]Cassidy and Henry (1987) England, Scotland, Wales.
[b]Montgomery and Pinder (1987) England and Wales.

A very similar rank order of the toxicity of antidepressants in overdosage was reported in another analysis based on National Health Service prescription data from England, Wales and Scotland for the period 1975–1984[14] (Table 12.2). There were significantly more deaths from overdose per million prescriptions with the older TCAs as a group than the average ratio for all antidepressants and the newer antidepressants had a significantly lower ratio of fatalities per million prescriptions than the average. These separate

Table 12.2. Antidepressants and overdose in the UK.

Drug	Fatal poisonings	Deaths per million prescriptions	Difference from all antidepressant $p<0.01$
Early TCAs introduced 1970 or before			
Dothiepin	533	50.0 (4.2)	Worse
Amitriptyline	1181	46.5 (2.6)	Worse
Nortriptyline	57	39.2 (10.2)	
Doxepin	102	31.3 (6.1)	
Imipramine	278	28.4 (3.3)	
Trimipramine	155	27.6 (4.3)	
Clomipramine	51	11.1 (3.0)	Safer
Protriptyline	6	10.3 (8.2)	Safer
Antidepressants introduced after 1973			
Maprotiline	83	37.6 (8.1)	
Trazodone	6	13.6 (10.9)	Safer
Viloxazine	2	9.4 (13.0)	Safer
Mianserin	30	5.6 (2.9)	Safer
Nomifensine	3	2.5 (2.8)	Safer
Lofepramine	0	0	Safer
All antidepressants	2551	34.9 (1.4)	

Adapted from Cassidy and Henry, 1987.

analyses have used different approaches and arrived at the same answer: the older TCAs, and in particular amitriptyline and dothiepin, are dangerous in overdose in comparison with other antidepressants.

Maprotiline, which has a tricyclic structure but which is misleadingly referred to as a tetracyclic, does not seem to have escaped the toxicity associated with the earlier TCAs. The recent report from a large study that maprotiline is associated with an increase in suicidal acts compared with placebo[15] suggests that it may actually provoke suicide attempts. It is possible that the higher rate of deaths from overdose seen with dothiepin and amitriptyline may also be a product of some feature of these drugs which provokes suicide attempts. Because of the extensive use of amitriptyline and dothiepin conclusions about their lethality in overdose can be made with greater confidence than with other less widely used antidepressants. Since both these drugs appear to be associated with more deaths per million prescriptions than other antidepressants, it seems likely that these two drugs have more inherent toxicity than others.

The older TCAs have significant effects on cardiac conduction, contractility and heart rate which may be seen even at therapeutic dosage. There is a correlation between plasma TCA levels and maximum QRS duration and intraventricular conduction delays occur more commonly with high levels of TCA.[16] ECG abnormalities commonly seen in TCA overdose include sinus tachycardia, prolongation of QT interval, intraventricular conduction defects and ST and T wave changes. The principal causes of death in TCA overdose are reported as being arrhythmias and depression of myocardial contractility.[9] The effects of TCA poisoning with these compounds are unpredictable and serious complications may be observed in some patients who ingest only small quantities of the drug.

Newer safer antidepressants

Of the newer TCAs only lofepramine appears to be clearly safer in overdose. A reliable estimate of toxicity in overdosage cannot be obtained until an antidepressant has been available for long enough to have been very widely used. The estimate of the probable safety of lofepramine provided by the analysis of Cassidy and Henry was based on only a short period after its recent introduction. More recent figures from the first 1.5 million prescriptions, which show there has been no death from overdose with lofepramine alone and only two in combination with other drugs, are in line with the earlier estimate of probable safety.[17]

Some of the newer non-tricyclic antidepressants, for example mianserin, have now been used very extensively and have proved to be significantly safer in overdose than the older TCAs. The importance of this aspect of safety of antidepressants is recognised and is taken into account in the development of new compounds. The new 5-HT uptake inhibitors, for example, are by and large lacking in cardiotoxic effects and while they have not been available for long enough to establish their safety in overdose in clinical use with the same confidence as for example, mianserin, there is every reason to expect them to be relatively safe. Monitoring of the first three million prescriptions of fluvoxamine has revealed no deaths from the drug alone and in some three million prescriptions of fluoxetine has shown one death from overdose with the drug alone. Both drugs therefore have good evidence of safety in overdose. This class of antidepressants has an additional advantage in overdose since nausea, which is a side effect associated with treatment, is dose related and overdose is therefore likely to be accompanied by vomiting.

INCREASED SUICIDE RATE WITH BENZODIAZEPINES AND ALCOHOL

The calculations of relative toxicity in overdose are based on the assumption that overdoses in a given population receiving antidepressants are randomly distributed. This may or may not be true. For example there is evidence that the assumption does not hold for patients taking benzodiazepines, which are reported to produce disinhibition and to cause an increase in both aggression and suicide attempts. Clinicians do well to heed the recent warnings from the

CSM and the Royal College of Psychiatrists cautioning doctors to be particularly careful in prescribing benzodiazepines to patients who are potentially suicidal.[18,19] Alcohol is reported likewise to increase the suicide rate by a rather similar mechanism and the number of deaths from drug overdosage associated with ingestion of alcohol is high.

REDUCED SUICIDE RATE AND 5-HT UPTAKE INHIBITORS?

The idea that all antidepressants are neutral in relation to suicidal thoughts and acts is an assumption which needs to be examined. One might ask if some antidepressants provoke suicide attempt: alternatively whether some antidepressants may reduce suicidal thoughts or impulses. It is even possible that some antidepressants may protect the individual from the expected toxicity of an overdose.

Clomipramine seems to differ from the older TCAs in that the death from overdose index is low in both the Montgomery and Pinder and the Cassidy and Henry analyses. This is surprising in view of the high number of deaths from adverse drug reactions (five per million prescriptions),[20] and the substantial levels of anticholinergic effects reported in clinical practice. Clomipramine is known to be rather toxic and appears to have greater danger than other TCAs in combination with MAOIs and deaths have been attributed to the combination of clomipramine and tranylcypramine.

One explanation has been that clomipramine has been selectively prescribed to obsessional patients who have a low risk of suicide. However clomipramine is also used by some physicians in treating categories of patients with a higher than normal risk of suicide, for example those with severe depression, and another explanation has to be be sought. Is there something specific to clomipramine which lowers the suicide rate? It is unlikely that clomipramine protects against the toxicity of other drugs since it has a high adverse drug inter-reaction profile. It is more likely that clomipramine reduces suicidal thoughts or impulses, thus protecting the individual from overdosing.

One test of this intriguing notion would be to see whether the suicidal thoughts or the attempt rates are selectively improved by clomipramine compared with other drugs in controlled studies. Unfortunately the number of patients included in controlled studies of clomipramine has been too small to provide adequate data on this issue. There is interesting indirect evidence from the studies of the 5-HT reuptake inhibitors which appear to reduce selectively suicidal thoughts compared with standard antidepressants.[21-23] This finding fits nicely with the hypothesis that there is a link between serotonin and impulse control. It may well be that 5-HT uptake inhibitors, including clomipramine, have a role in reducing impulsivity and may consequently reduce the suicidal attempt rate.

TAKING ACCOUNT OF THE RISK IN OVERDOSE

The level of toxicity of amitriptyline and dothiepin is unacceptable in drugs that are used to treat potentially suicidal patients. If deaths from adverse drug reactions were reported at this level they would be a major cause for concern. Nomifensine, for example, was withdrawn by the manufacturers when seven deaths from immunoallergic reactions per million prescriptions were reported.[24]

Conventional techniques of reducing the risk such as blister packing the medication, supplying in small quantities, and selecting patients with care, have clearly not been sufficiently widely taken up. The mean number of deaths from overdose with TCAs in the UK is 38.5 per million prescriptions and there are grounds for withholding these drugs from suicidally prone patients treated in the community setting unless supplied in very small quantities or unless the support of friends and relatives can be enlisted to look after medication.

It is of course not possible to eliminate the risk completely and it is reasonable to suggest a safety standard for antidepressants. More than 10 deaths per million patients treated would represent a drug that is not so safe, more than 20 deaths per million a dangerous drug, more than 30 deaths per million a very dangerous drug only to be used with great caution, and more than 40 deaths per million an unacceptable risk. Based on this calculation the

Table 12.3. Antidepressants and overdose.

Relatively safe
Less than 10 deaths per million prescriptions:
lofepramine, mianserin, fluvoxamine, fluoxetine, viloxazine

Not so safe
More than 10 deaths per million:
clomipramine, protriptyline, trazadone

Dangerous
More than 20 deaths per million:
phenelzine

Very dangerous
More than 30 deaths per million:
maprotiline, imipramine, doxepin

Unacceptable risk
More than 40 deaths per million:
dothiepin, amitriptyline

relatively safe drugs in the UK would be mianserin, lofepramine, fluvoxamine and fluoxetine and viloxazine (Table 12.3). Since there is no evidence that dothiepin or amitriptyline, which have an unacceptable risk, are more effective than the newer antidepressants the choice of antidepressant must be made on the basis of relative risk. The level of toxicity in overdosage of the older TCAs should have the effect of relegating them to second line treatment, the newer safer antidepressants being preferred in patients who are treated at home.

REFERENCES

1. Kennedy P.F. and Kreitman N. (1973). An epidemiological survey of parasuicide ('attempted suicide') in general practice. *British Journal of Psychiatry*, **123**, 23–34.
2. Kreitman N. (1977). *Parasuicide*. Wiley, Chichester.
3. Guze S.B. and Robins E. (1970). Suicide among primary affective disorders. *British Journal of Psychiatry*, **117**, 437–438.
4. Sims, A.C.P. (1988). The mortality associated with depression. *International Clinical Psychopharmacology*, **3** (Suppl. 1), 1–14.
5. Tsuang M.T., Woolson J.F.F. and Fleming J.A. (1980). Premature deaths in schizophrenia and affective disorders. *Archives of General Psychiatry*, **37**, 979–983.
6. Prescott L.F. and Highley M.S. (1985). Drugs prescribed for self poisoners. *British Medical Journal*, **290**, 1633–1636.
7. Montgomery S.A. and Tyrer P.J. (1988). Benzodiazepines: time to withdraw. *Journal of the Royal College of General Practitioners*, **38**, 146–147.
8. Gardner D.L. and Cowdry R.J.W. (1985). Alprazolam-induced dyscontrol in borderline personality disorder. *American Journal of Psychiatry*, **141**, 98–100.
9. Frommer D.A. Kulig K.W., Marx J.A. and Rumack B. (1987). Tricyclic antidepressant overdose. *Journal of the American Medical Association*, **257**, 521–526.
10. Crome P. and Newman B. (1979). Fatal tricyclic antidepressant poisoning. *Journal of the Royal Society of Medicine*, **72**, 649–653.
11. Park J. and Proudfoot A.T. (1977). Acute poisoning with maprotiline hydrochloride. *British Medical Journal*, **1**, 1573.
12. Inman W.H.W. (1988). Blood disorders and suicide in patients taking mianserin or amitriptyline. *Lancet*, **i**, 90–92.
13. Montgomery S.A. and Pinder R.M. (1987). Do some antidepressants promote suicide? *Psychopharmacology*, **92**, 265–266.
14. Cassidy S. and Henry J. (1987). Fatal toxicity of antidepressant drugs in overdose. *British Medical Journal*, **295**, 1021–1024.
15. Rouillon F., Phillips R., Serrurier D., Ansart E. and Gerard M.J. (1989). Rechutes de depression unipolaire et efficacite de la maprotiline. *L'Encephale*, **15**, 527–534.
16. Spiker D. G., Weiss A.N., Chang S.S., Ruwitch J.F. and Biggs J.T. (1975). Tricyclic antidepressant overdose: clinical presentation and plasma levels. *Clinical Pharmacology and Therapeutics*, **18**, 539–546.
17. Montgomery, S.A., Lambert T. and Lynch S. (1988). The risk of suicide with antidepressants. *International Clinical Psychopharmacology*, **3** (Suppl. 1), 15–24.

18. Committee for the Safety of Medicines (1988). Benzodiazepines, dependence and withdrawal symptoms. *Current Problems*, **21**.

19. Priest R.G. and Montgomery S.A. (1988). Benzodiazepines and dependence. *Royal College Psychiatrists Bulletin*, **12**, 107–109.

20. Committee for the Safety of Medicines Update (1985). Adverse reactions to antidepressants. *British Medical Journal*, **291**, 1638.

21. Montgomery S.A., McAuley R., Rani S.J., Roy D. and Montgomery D.B. (1981). A double blind comparison of zimelidine and amitriptyline in endogenous depression. *Acta Psychiatrica Scandinavica*, **290** (Suppl.), 314–327.

22. Muijen, M., Roy D., Silverstone T., Mehmet A. and Christie M. (1988). A comparative clinical trial of fluoxetine, mianserin and placebo with depressed outpatients. *Acta Psychiatrica Scandinavica*, **78**, 380–390.

23. Committee for the Safety of Medicines Update (1986). Withdrawal of nomifensine. *British Medical Journal*, **293**, 41.

24. Wakelin J. (1988). The role of serotonin in depression and suicide. *Advances in Biological Psychiatry*, **17**, 70–83Y.

13

How Long Should Antidepressant Treatment Continue?

Treating depression involves more than simply selecting the right antidepressant and waiting for the symptoms to subside: it is now recognised that the treatment should continue in all patients for some time after apparent response to consolidate the recovery. This important aspect of treatment seems often to be neglected by doctors particularly in primary care settings, and courses of treatment are too short. This further period of treatment to cement the response is a maintenance or continuation phase of the treatment of the acute episode of depression. In patients who have recurrent episodes of depression long-term prophylactic treatment after this continuation phase aims to reduce the likelihood of further episodes of depression.

CONTINUATION TREATMENT

If antidepressants are withdrawn too promptly following a response of the acute episode about half of the patients will suffer a return of their depressive symptoms during the next few months. This return of depressive symptoms occurs as frequently in those suffering from depressive illness for the first time as in those with recurrent depression and should properly be regarded as inadequate treatment of the acute episode.

It is thought that while antidepressants improve the acute symptoms of depression, usually within 4–6 weeks, the underlying illness may take longer to resolve. It is as if a period of frailty follows the response of the acute symptoms during which the patient, although apparently symptom free, remains vulnerable and prone to suffer a relapse or return of the original depression. Antidepressants should therefore not be stopped as soon as response has been observed but should be continued to maintain the response and protect the patient during this period. An indirect analogy may be drawn with treatment of infections with an antibiotic where the first couple of days usually sees the resolution of the fever but a full course of treatment is required to properly eliminate the infection and prevent its return once treatment is stopped.

Is continuation treatment really necessary?

The evidence for the efficacy of antidepressants compared with placebo in reducing relapse in the period of recovery following the acute episode is impressive. The need for continuation treatment has been established in placebo-controlled trials with the reference TCAs amitriptyline and imipramine. To judge from the published literature, other TCAs, such as dothiepin and doxepin, have not been formally assessed in this respect. Three separate studies have shown that patients treated with amitriptyline following response of the acute episode of depression have significantly less relapse of their depressive symptoms in the ensuing months than patients treated with placebo.[1,2,3] A further study showed a similar advantage for amitriptyline compared with diazepam.[4] Two studies have also shown the efficacy of imipramine compared with placebo in this continuation phase of treatment but one did not.[1,5,6]

The consistency of these significant results compared with placebo and in others with reference TCAs, supports the notion that a period of continuation or maintenance treatment is required with all antidepressants following the resolution of acute symptoms of depression. The high relapse rate seen in patients who had apparently recovered from their acute depression and who were then treated with placebo is a clear warning of the continuing vulnerability after initial symptomatic response. Efficacy in consolidating response now needs to be formally tested and it would be unwise to assume that all drugs that have been shown to be effective in acute treatment necessarily have long-term efficacy.

How long?

An adequate course of treatment will continue sufficiently long after the apparent response of the acute symptoms to ensure that the depressive episode is fully resolved. One view is that in order to be sure of best effect continuation therapy has therefore to be maintained until the episode would be expected to have passed without intervention. Since it may be difficult to gauge how long an episode is likely to last with any particular patient some general guidelines are needed.

The need for a prolonged treatment period with antidepressants after apparent recovery was established in studies varying in length from 2–8 months. The relapses tended to occur in the first months after premature discontinuation of antidepressant treatment, too soon for them to be the manifestation of new episodes. There is a consistent relapse rate in these studies of some 50% in the 4–6 months continuation period on early substitution to placebo and this compares with a relapse rate of 20% on active treatment. It seems that the risk diminishes the longer the patient is kept on the antidepressant and that relapse is less frequent if patients have remained well during treatment with antidepressants for at least 4 months following response before treatment is discontinued.

A difference of this magnitude is a compelling reason for the practitioner to encourage patients to complete an adequate course of antidepressant treatment. In order to be sure that the depressive episode has passed, treatment will have to continue for a minimum of 4 months after the acute symptoms have resolved. The advice would be to continue treatment if possible even longer, say for six months, which would ensure that a proportion of patients made a full recovery who otherwise would not have done. Most patients are currently being undertreated for their depression since the average duration of treatment with an antidepressant in the UK is of the order of 1 month.

Which patients?

Fifty percent of all patients have a relapse on discontinuation of antidepressant but unfortunately we have no sure way of predicting who these unlucky patients might be. None of the studies of continuation treatment have been able to identify a constellation of symptoms which predict the likelihood of early relapse. Even knowledge of the particular patient's history and length of previous episodes does not help a great deal since the duration of episodes may lengthen slightly with recurrence,[7] some depressions run a chronic course, and intervention with antidepressant treatment will have obscured the natural length of the episodes.

It does however appear that if there have been any depressive symptoms, even mild ones, during a continuation treatment phase of at least 4 months following response of the acute episode then patients have a higher chance of relapse on discontinuation of the antidepressant. Only when a patient has been symptom free for this length of time can the practitioner begin to feel more confident that the episode has resolved. Even then it has to be remembered that the majority of relapses occur in the first 2 months following early discontinuation of the antidepressant and particularly close follow up during this period will be needed. Table 13.1 gives guidelines for continuation treatment.

Table 13.1. Continuation of acute treatment.

1. All depression, first time or recurrent needs a full 6 month period of treatment. Continuation treatment helps reduce the chance of a set back.
2. If treatment is continued at least 4 months after response risk of return of symptoms is reduced.
3. Full explanation to the patient helps compliance. If the patient understands the need for continuation treatment compliance improves.
   Maintenance treatment helps reduce the chance of a set back.
4. Antidepressants do not cause dependence. Patients find it all too easy to stop taking them.

PROPHYLACTIC TREATMENT AND THE PREVENTION OF FUTURE EPISODES OF DEPRESSION

Estimates of the proportion of first time depression which become recurrent vary but if patients are followed up over long periods a very high proportion are seen to develop recurrent depression.[8,9] There is however general agreement that the majority of unipolar depression is recurrent[10,11] and the possible efficacy of antidepressants in reducing the risk of new episodes is therefore of great importance.

In view of the size of the problem it is perhaps surprising that so few studies of the prophylactic efficacy of antidepressants in reducing the risk of new episodes had until recently been undertaken. In the relative absence of evidence from controlled studies clinicians have tended to assume that if an antidepressant is effective in the acute illness it will also be effective in prophylaxis. This assumption would help to explain why some of the most widely prescribed antidepressants for long-term usage have not been adequately investigated for this form of efficacy.

The difference between continuation and prophylactic treatment

There is a distinction to be made between efficacy in continuation treatment and efficacy in reducing the chance of new episodes of depression. The re-emergence of symptoms which is seen in some 50% of patients if antidepressants are stopped prematurely after the acute symptoms of depression have resolved represents inadequate treatment of the original episode and should not be taken as the appearance of a new episode of depressive illness. To find out if an antidepressant reduces the occurrence of new episodes of depression, efficacy is tested in patients who have been free of symptoms for a defined period long enough to cover the full recovery period.

Which antidepressants have prophylactic efficacy?

Some of the early studies on the prophylactic efficacy of antidepressants did not pay as much attention to the necessary methodology as is now thought appropriate. The evidence from these early studies is therefore not as convincing as the more recent studies which have paid close attention to the need for a defined symptom free period after response, a sufficient recurrence of episodes in the group studied, and, most important of all, the inclusion of sufficient numbers of patients to adequately test prophylactic efficacy. Most of the studies have examined efficacy in the 1–2 year range and it is clear that very few patients have not relapsed during placebo treatment after 18 months to 2 years. This makes it difficult to properly test prophylactic efficacy in a controlled study after 2 years because of the small number of patients who have not relapsed on placebo by then. This high relapse rate on placebo makes it clear that prophylaxis, if undertaken, should continue for a very long period, possibly for life.

Tricyclic antidepressants

The evidence for the prophylactic efficacy of amitriptyline may be tentatively accepted although based on only two early long-term studies, both of them small and flawed.[12,13] The studies on imipramine are more convincing and there are three adequate studies which found efficacy.[6,14,15] The only study which has not found efficacy was a very small one.[16] Some indication of prophylatic efficacy may be provided in a study of continuation treatment over a one year period with maprotiline[17] but efficacy was not calculated in the continuation and prophylactic phases separately. The prophylactic efficacy of other TCAs is assumed rather than tested. Nortriptyline, for example, was not found to have efficacy in a recent placebo-controlled study in the elderly which found that phenelzine was effective.[18] Long-term treatment with some of the more widely used TCAs such as dothiepin and doxepin requires an act of faith which is not without danger. It would be wiser to switch to treatments with proven prophylactic efficacy.

5-HT uptake inhibitors

The recent studies on 5-HT uptake inhibitors are better designed and show convincing prophylactic efficacy. A large prophylactic efficacy has been carried out comparing fluoxetine with placebo in a 1 year study.[19] Fluoxetine showed a highly significant advantage compared with placebo in reducing recurrences of unipolar depression with twice as many patients suffering a new episode of depression during placebo treatment as during treatment with fluoxetine. The efficacy of zimelidine, the first of these compounds to be introduced, was shown in a very well conducted 18 month study[20] but the impact of this finding was lost with the subsequent withdrawal of the drug from the market. A significant effect in reducing new episodes has also been shown with a third 5-HT uptake inhibitor, sertraline, in a placebo-controlled study of continuation treatment with a short period of prophylactic treatment which showed efficacy.[21]

The positive results of the studies of 5-HT uptake inhibitors greatly strengthen the case for the prophylactic efficacy of antidepressants in recurrent unipolar depression. The implication of the prophylactic studies, particularly those recent ones which have used more stringent methodology is that prophylactic treatment of recurrent unipolar depression should be continued for long periods of time.

Lithium

Lithium was investigated in placebo-controlled studies principally in the prophylaxis of bipolar depressive illness where it is regarded as the drug of choice. However sufficient numbers of individuals with unipolar illness were included in these studies to permit a metanalysis which indicates efficacy.[22] This was supported by one positive reasonably sized placebo-controlled study and another tiny study but not by a third fair sized study.[10,13,14] On balance the efficacy of lithium is accepted by many, but antidepressants, particularly the newer ones, would be a favoured treatment because of the ease of prescribing, the reduced side effects, the lack of the need for plasma level monitoring, and the relative safety.

Do all patients with recurrent depression need prophylaxis?

The longitudinal studies in unipolar depression indicate that there is a tendency for episodes to occur more frequently and the duration of remission to be reduced with each further episode. It is possible that in later life this may stabilise to a more constant recurrence rate. For any individual patient the decision as to whether to embark on prophylactic treatment will relate to the projection, based on the history, of the next expected episode. The early studies on prophylaxis were mostly carried out in patients who had suffered from three or more episodes of depression. However in the recent studies such as on fluoxetine and zimelidine it appears that patients with two episodes of depression in 5 years will probably benefit from prophylaxis. This is reflected in the recent World Health Organization Consensus Statement suggesting that it is appropriate to consider prophylactic treatment for any recently recovered patient with one previous episode of depression in the previous 5 years. The advantage of this criterion is that it is easy to understand, identifies the group with a substantial predicted recurrent morbidity, and may be used very simply in the clinical setting. Clinicians would be wise to advise patients as completely as possible of the risk of recurrence in order that they may make an informed decision about taking medication for long periods of time to reduce the chances of further illness.

Dosage in maintenance and prophylaxis

It is widely held that the dose needed for prophylactic treatment in recovered depressed patients need not be as high as that needed to treat the acute depression. However the studies which have found prophylactic efficacy have almost all used full recommended doses. It is possible that lower doses may indeed be effective but there is insufficient evidence to recommend them. The evidence for a lower dose in the maintenance phase of therapy following the response of the acute symptoms is rather scarce but does at least suggest that the dose for amitriptyline and maprotiline need not be as high as the standard recommended dose. In the maprotiline study[17] both the half standard dose, 75 mg, and the quarter dose appeared to be effective compared with placebo although the half dose had the best outcome. Both doses, despite apparent efficacy in long-term treatment, were associated with increased incidence of suicide attempts which is both disturbing an unexplained. The main reason for using a lower dose is that the side effects are often sufficiently high to compromise compliance. This is certainly true with the tricyclic antidepressants but for the newer antidepressants which have fewer side effects there seems little reason not to use the full dose.

ARE THERE DRAWBACKS TO LONG-TERM ANTIDEPRESSANT TREATMENT?

If an antidepressant is to be used for many months patients and practitioners will be particularly concerned to know about the possible level of toxicity and whether additional unwanted side effects will result from long-term use. Patients are also often worried about the possibility of becoming dependent on antidepressants, a worry which has been exacerbated by current concerns over the dependence potential of benzodiazepines since there is not always a clear distinction in the patient's mind between tranquillisers and antidepressants. One of the advantages of the more stringent testing now demanded in establishing the efficacy of new antidepressants is that much more is known about their possible disadvantages. New potential antidepressants have to be tested for efficacy and for safety not only in short acute treatment studies but also in long-term therapy.

Tolerance and withdrawal effects

Dependence

Fortunately dependence is not a problem with antidepressants but patients sometimes need a great deal of reassurance about this. There is usually no difficulty in stopping treatment and the main problem is discontinuing the drug too early because the patient feels well. Abruptly stopping treatment with TCAs can however be associated with some troublesome but short-lived symptoms which are thought to arise from the action of the TCAs on the cholinergic system. Some patients complain of anxiety, sleep disturbance and dreaming when TCAs are stopped suddenly, and a number of cases of overactivity have been described. These symptoms are unlikely to be confused with a relapse of the depression as they resolve rapidly. It does not appear to be a general problem but gradual reduction of dosage of TCAs before stopping is advisable.

In the large prophylactic study of fluoxetine medication was withdrawn abruptly in those patients who were subsequently treated with placebo in the study. There were no signs of withdrawal phenomena either of the sort seen with benzodiazepines or of the short transient increase in anxiety seen on withdrawal of the TCAs. The process of withdrawal of fluoxetine, however abruptly done, is softened by the long half life of its active metabolite, the levels of which gradually decline after stopping the drug thereby achieving in effect a gradual withdrawal.

Tolerance

Tolerance to side effects is observed with all antidepressants. On a constant dose the side effects are most obvious in the first few days of treatment and thereafter seem to be tolerated better. In contrast efficacy takes time to be evident and then remains constant. In long-term treatment the power of prophylactic effect remains constant and there is no need to increase the dose with time. The appearance of new side effects or worsening of side effects during longer term treatment does not seem to be a problem with antidepressants.

The anticholinergic effects of the tricyclic antidepressants do not of course go away during treatment and in choosing which antidepressant to use for a particular patient the possibility of these and the cardiotoxic effects will need to be borne in mind. Some patients who have difficulty adjusting to the side effects they experience with the older TCAs, such as weight gain or persistent dry mouth, may be understandably unwilling to continue treatment over a period of months and the new 5-HT uptake inhibitors which have fewer associated unwanted effects are likely to be a more acceptable and effective choice of long-term treatment.

Bipolar illness

In bipolar affective disorders, where there are manic as well as depressive episodes in the history, lithium has been thoroughly investigated in placebo-controlled studies and its efficacy in reducing subsequent episodes of illness is established. The consistency with which the prophylactic effect of lithium is seen can leave no doubt that this is the treatment of choice. Antidepressants appear less helpful than lithium in the prophylaxis of bipolar depression because they are associated with the precipitation of mania in a significant proportion of cases. This phenomenon appears to occur with all antidepressants not just particular compounds.

Treatment of bipolar patients will usually have been instituted during psychiatric in- or outpatient care and stabilised in an outpatient lithium clinic. However since these patients will continue taking lithium effectively for the rest of their lives follow up is mostly done in the community. Lithium is a troublesome drug to prescribe as it has to be monitored to keep the plasma level within a narrow range to avoid high levels associated with increased toxicity and yet maintain a therapeutic level. Unfortunately these patients do not always stay well, whether because they stop taking their medication or because the medication fails to maintain its efficacy.

Carbamazepine

Carbemazapine may be helpful in the prophylaxis of bipolar disorders but as yet the evidence is rather slight in comparison with that for lithium. There are suggestions that carbamazepine may be particularly helpful in bipolar patients with very rapid cycles and in bipolars with bizarre presentations and schizoaffective features. In individuals with a history of depression and epilepsy carbamazepine may have an important role. Like lithium, carbamazepine is difficult to manage in that it also requires plasma level monitoring. There is a rather high incidence of skin reactions including the dangerous Stevens–Johnson syndrome. The evidence of efficacy in unipolar depression is slight and the dangers too great to recommend it compared with those antidepressants where efficacy and safety have been established.

PERSUADING THE PATIENT TO CONTINUE TREATMENT

Patients suffering from depression are often reluctant to accept the need for drug treatment for their illness and persuading them to continue antidepressant treatment for long enough to obtain the best effect can be a problem. They may fear becoming dependent on drugs and they often cannot understand the need for continued medication when their symptoms have resolved. The idea of continuing to visit the doctor for follow up when they have felt well for some time may seem perverse.

The practitioner's task is one of careful persuasion and one of the best means at his disposal is to provide patients with information about the course of the illness and about the likelihood of relapse if treatment is discontinued early. There is clear evidence from the placebo-controlled studies that the rate of new episodes is halved by effective long-term antidepressants in patients with recurrent depression. This is information that patients need to have to help them make an informed decision about the need for continuing treatment prophylactically (Table 13.2).

Table 13.2.   Recurrent depression and prophylaxis.

1. Reducing the chance of a new episode of depression by at least 50% will reduce incidence of dangerous illness
2. Full explanation helps patient make decision
3. Two episodes in 5 years = clear cut need for prophylaxis
4. Length of treatment if needed is prolonged

The aim is to achieve a balanced decision which takes the unwillingness to go on to prophylactic treatment and the likelihood of further episodes into account. The decision will also need to take into account the severity of illness and degree of incapacity and risk the illness brings. Depression should never be underestimated in this respect: it is an illness with substantial morbidity and mortality from both suicide and concomitant physical illness. The depressive illness is slow to respond to treatment during which relationships, jobs, and life itself are all at risk. Any treatment over the long-term which is able to reduce the chances of unnecessary extra episodes of this destructive and unpleasant disease should be worth the inconvenience of taking regular medication.

REFERENCES

1. Mindham R.H.S., Howland C. and Shepherd M. (1973). An evaluation of continuation therapy with tricyclic antidepressants in depressive illness. *Psychological Medicine*, **3**, 5–17.
2. Klerman G.L., Dimascio A., Weissman M., Prusoff B. and Paykel E. (1974). Treatment of depression by drugs and psychotherapy. *American Journal of Psychiatry*, **131**, 186–191.
3. Stein M., Rickels K. and Weise C.C. (1980). Maintenance therapy with amitriptyline: A controlled trial. *American Journal of Psychiatry*, **137**, 370–371.
4. Kay D.W.K., Fahy T. and Garside, R.F. (1970). A seven-month double-blind trial of amitriptyline and diazepam in ECT-treated depressed patients. *British Journal of Psychiatry*, **117**, 667–671.

5. Seager C.P. and Bird R.L. (1962). Imipramine with electrical treatment in depression – a controlled trial. *Journal of Mental Science*, **108**, 704–707.
6. Prien R., Klett C.J. and Caffey E.M. (1973). Lithium carbonate and imipramine in the prevention of affective episodes. *Archives of General Psychiatry*, **29**, 420–425.
7. Kielholz P. (1959). *Klinik, Differentialdiagnostik und Therapie der depressiven Zustandsbilder.* Geigy, Basel.
8. Angst J. (1973). The course of monopolar depression and bipolar psychoses. *Psychiatria Neurologia Neurochirurgia*, **76**, 489–500.
9. Coryell W.S. and Winokur G. (1982). Course and outcome. In: *Handbook of Affective Disorders* (Ed. E.S. Paykel), Churchill Livingstone, Edinburgh, pp. 93–106.
10. Nystrom S. (1979). Depressions: factors related to ten-year prognosis. *Acta Psychiatrica Scandinavica*, **60**, 225–238.
11. Zis A. P. and Goodwin, F. K. (1979). Major affective disorder as a recurrent illness: a critical review. *Archives of General Psychiatry*, **36**, 835–839.
12. Coppen A., Ghose K., Montgomery S., Rama Rao V.A., Bailey J. and Jorgensen A. (1978). Continuation therapy with amitriptyline in depression. *British Journal of Psychiatry*, **133**, 28–33.
13. Glen A.I.M., Johnson A.L. and Shepherd M (1984). Continuation therapy with lithium and amitriptyline in unipolar depressive illness: a randomized, double-blind, controlled trial. *Psychological Medicine*, **14**, 37–50.
14. Prien R., Kupfer D.J., Mansky P.A., Small J.G., Tuason V.B., Voss C.B. and Johnson W.E. (1984). Drug therapy in the prevention of recurrences in unipolar and bipolar affective disorders. *Archives of General Psychiatry*, **41**, 1096–1104.
15. Frank E., Kupfer D.J., Perel J.M. (1989). Early recurrence in unipolar depression. *Archives of General Psychiatry*, **46**, 397–400.
16. Kane J.M., Quitken F. M., Rifkin A., Ramos-Lorenzi J.R., Nayak D.D. and Howard A. (1982). Lithium carbonate and imipramine in the prophylaxis of unipolar and bipolar II illness. *Archives of General Psychiatry*, **39**, 1065–1069.
17. Rouillon F., Phillips R., Serrurier D., Ansart E. and Gerard M. J. (1989). Prophylactic efficacy of maprotiline on relapses of unipolar depression. *L'encephale*, **15**, 527–534.
18. Georgotas A., McCue R.E. and Cooper T.B. (1989). A placebo-controlled comparison of nortriptyline and phenelzine in maintenance therapy of elderly depressed patients. *Archives of General Psychiatry*, **46**, 783–786.
19. Montgomery S.A., Dufour H., Brion S., Gailledreau J., Laqueille X., Ferrey G., Moron P., Parant-Lucena N., Singer L., Danion J.M., Beuzen J.N. and Pierredon M.A. (1988). The prophylactic efficacy of fluoxetine in unipolar depression. *British Journal of Psychiatry*, **153** (Suppl. 3), 69–76.
20. Bjork K. (1983). The efficacy of zimelidine in preventing depressive episodes in recurrent major depressive disorders—a double-blind placebo-controlled study. *Acta Psychiatrica Scandinavica*, **68**, 182–189.
21. Doogan D.P. and Caillard V. (1988). Sertraline in the prevention of relapse in major depression. *Psychopharmacology*, **96** (Suppl.), 271.
22. Schou M. (1979). Lithium as a prophylactic agent in unipolar affective illness. *Archives of General Psychiatry*, **36**, 849–851.

14

Getting the Best From Antidepressants

People who have recovered from a depressive illness describe the dark clouds of pessimism and incompetence which overwhelm them, the loss of motivation and the inability to do or enjoy anything. These features of the illness can be an obstacle to treatment which needs to be overcome. Many people are frightened of antidepressants which have the reputation of being heavy undesirable drugs which should be stopped as soon as possible. They may be reluctant to rely on drugs to treat the depression which they frequently see as a psychological weakness. For these reasons, antidepressants are frequently used in doses which are too low and in courses of treatment which are too short. The doctor clearly has a difficult task to counter the patient's reluctance to take antidepressants and to get the best out of the treatment.

For those families who have a serious prejudice against psychiatric illness in general or depression in particular, it is sometimes helpful to avoid the diagnosis altogether. In France, for example, the diagnosis of inhibition of the nervous system is sometimes given and antidepressants are prescribed. Another device which can be helpful is to diagnose tiredness or exhaustion. I quote here an example I have heard used successfully: 'I am afraid your wife is overtired and seriously run down and needs something to revitalise her nervous system. It has taken some time to reach this state and it will take 6 weeks or more to improve matters and a further few months to stabilise the energy levels'.

GETTING THE BEST OUT OF TREATMENT

Belief in the treatment

The best treatment is the one that is believed in, and the belief must be shared by the doctor and the patient. The doctor has to convince the patient that he knows the chosen antidepressant works, not always an easy task in the face of the characteristic pessimism of depression. Unless the patient is convinced the extra placebo effect on top of the pharmacological effect of the drug will be lost. If the doctor manages to convey his belief in treatment the confidence in the drug should carry over into the patient's response.

Caring about the antidepressant is a key to improved response. The careless prescription of an antidepressant 'You'll soon feel better and a little antidepressant might not do you any harm' is unlikely to improve the response. If an old drug is used it helps patients to be told it is 'tried and tested' or 'the one in which I have most confidence'; or if a new one is prescribed that it is 'the latest and best'. It is important to care about which antidepressant is chosen and it is important to convey that concern.

Support and reassurance

Those with depression lose perspective and describe how they worry endlessly over every little thing. They seek reassurance which often appears to be poorly received although when they recover they are often able to tell you how they had been helped. Recognising the need for supportive reassurance is an important contribution to recovery and with this in mind relatives and friends should be encouraged to form a network of understanding and concerned support for the individual while he or she is depressed.

Accessibility

The negative, defeated attitude of depressed individuals prevents them from making an accurate appraisal of events. They will often do the wrong thing. They may perceive a delay in consultation while an appointment is made as confirmation of their ideas that they do not deserve to be seen, and they may not return for treatment. This is one of the reasons why the depressed individual should always be seen as soon as possible. Likewise, when treatment has been started it is important to respond rapidly to sudden deterioration in the patient's condition. Patients may despair when without warning the depression, which had improved, apparently returns. At these moments patients need, and should be given, prompt reassurance that the setback is temporary so that they should persist with treatment.

Information about the course of response

Patients nowadays are better informed than they used to be and expect to be given information about their illness and treatment. One of the best means of improving response the practitioner has, is to encourage a cooperative effort by providing the patient with information on all aspects of treatment.

It will certainly help if the doctor explains the nature of response in depression. Many patients, very reasonably but quite unrealistically, expect to feel better the moment the first tablet is swallowed. Unless they are forewarned that depression responds slowly they may be too discouraged to continue treatment when they continue to feel ill. It is well worth warning them that they will probably feel worse before they feel better; that they may have to adjust to the side effects of an antidepressant before any real benefit begins to show. Realistic support acknowledging the time it will take to see a response helps patients to adjust to this long haul and continue the treatment.

Patients will also be less discouraged by the uneven course of response if it is explained that depressive symptoms may come and go in the course of treatment. Some patients are understandably immensely relieved at the first response which they assume means the end of their depression and then are devastatingly dejected if there is a sudden reversal. Explanation at the start of treatment that progress may follow a 'two steps forward and one step back' pattern, and reassurance if there is a setback will both be needed. Cautious optimism in explaining that the direction overall is what counts and that a small reversal is part of the response may help to keep the patient going.

Improve compliance with treatment

One of the reasons why treatment is sometimes ineffective is that people who are prescribed antidepressants fail to take them at all, do not keep to the treatment regime, or stop taking them prematurely. This is a problem of some dimension as studies of compliance with medication in depressed patients in general practice have shown. In one study, for example, 68% of patients were no longer taking the antidepressant drugs that had been prescribed for them after 4 weeks.[1]

Prescribing medication which is not taken fails to treat the patient's depression, is wasteful of drugs, and leads to accumulation of unused drugs which, especially in an illness like depression, may be used later in a suicidal attempt. The reasons for non-compliance therefore need to be understood and ways around the problem to be found. A variety of reasons may be given for failing to take medication and these include the patient's perceived lack of response, the patient's considering themselves well, concerns about what the effects of the drugs might be, the experience of unacceptable side effects, and, particularly in the elderly, being prescribed a treatment regime which was too complicated to manage.

Adverse experience of drugs causes loss of confidence

The side effects of treatment cause many patients to stop taking antidepressants. The older tricyclic antidepressants are only too well known for their side effects which are sometimes frightening to patients, particularly if they have not been forewarned. The degree of discomfort caused by the dry mouth, blurred vision, daytime sedation, and loss of concentration, varies with the individual but some find 'the side effects worse than the disease'. Many of these patients stop taking the medication after a few days and do not return to treatment.

There are a number of strategies that can be employed to help the patient to comply with treatment.

Choose antidepressants with fewer side effects. The most obvious course is to avoid prescribing the antidepressants with the most unacceptable side effects. In one typical general practice study of antidepressants 18% of patients treated with TCAs withdrew from treatment and a further 24% had their dose limited because of intolerable side effects.[1] Most of the newer drugs, e.g. mianserin, lofepramine, trazadone, fluvoxamine, and fluoxetine have significantly fewer and less severe side effects than the TCAs and are more easily accepted (see Tables 14.1 and 14.2). The loss of side effects with these newer antidepressants does not reflect any loss of efficacy and they should therefore be the treatment of choice. Maprotiline and dothiepin which have

Table 14.1.   Antidepressants with marked unwanted effects.

Drug	Side effects	Deaths in overdose
Amitriptyline	Very sedative	+++
Dothiepin	Very sedative	+++
Maprotiline	Sedative	++
Trimipramine	Very sedative	+
Clomipramine	Sedative	−
Imipramine	Mildly sedative	++

Start low
Raise dose to effective level as soon as possible

Table 14.2.   Antidepressants with fewer unwanted effects.

Drug	Side effects	Deaths in overdose
Mianserin	Sedative	−
Trazadone	Sedative	−
Viloxazine	Neutral	−
Lofepramine	Neutral	−
Fluvoxamine	Neutral	−
Fluoxetine	Neutral	−

Start at effective dose

been advertised as having fewer side effects turn out to have serious problems, e.g. convulsions and cardiotoxicity as evidenced by the deaths in overdosage. Fluvoxamine, for which the standard recommended dose is probably too high, may cause nausea and vomiting. It is possible to reduce the impact of some of the predicted side effects by choosing the appropriate dosage regime. Nausea may be reduced by taking the antidepressant with a meal. Likewise a sedative antidepressant is best taken before sleeping.

Dosage. Many depressed patients treated in general practice receive very low, subtherapeutic doses of antidepressants and others, who are prescribed the full standard dose, fail to take them as prescribed .[2-4] One of the reasons why low doses are used, particularly in general practice, is the difficulty in persuading ambulatory patients to accept the full dose. To reduce the discomfort of side effects which might make patients discontinue treatment it is best to start with a low dose and escalate slowly. This device can be successful even with the unpleasant side effects of the TCAs so that with time the appropriate recommended therapeutic dose can be reached. The delay in reaching the right dose is the price paid for keeping the individual in treatment. It is very important to continue to raise the dose and to reach the full effective dose as quickly as possible. Although it is tempting to stop early if there is a partial remission this could be dangerous. A half treated depressive is at great risk and, while it is difficult to be sure, it is thought that suicide is more likely in these patients. The other problem is that some inadequately treated depressives embark on a career of chronic depression, inappropriately called resistant depression or dysthymia.

Explain the possible side effects. Forewarned is forearmed. Explaining the likely side effects to the patient, before he or she finds out by experience,

Table 14.3. Common side effects of which patients should be warned.

TCAs	Anticholinergic side effects: dry mouth, constipation, tremor Sedation and concentration difficulties Care needed with operating machinery Dangers of driving during treatment
Viloxazine	Nausea
Fluvoxamine	Nausea and vomiting Some initial increase in nervousness
Fluoxetine	Mild nausea Some initial increase in nervousness
Mianserin	Sedation
Trazadone	Sedation Nausea

can help them to tolerate what would otherwise be disturbing side effects. Explanation needs to be kept within sensible limits as too much detail of the rarer effects may discourage patients from even starting treatment. An explanation, brief or detailed according to the patient's needs, of the main side effects and the course of evolution and decline is often all that is needed to reassure the patient that the side effects experienced are an expected part of the pattern of treatment and nothing unusual (Table 14.3).

The positive aspect of side effects. It is often possible to turn the appearance of side effects to advantage in reinforcing the efficacy of the treatment: 'Good, it means the treatment is getting to where it is needed'; 'This tells us that the drug is beginning to work'. At the same time if a patient wants to know more there is no reason to be afraid of revealing the limits of our knowledge. 'We do not know quite how it works but we know that it does'. Some of the side effects may indeed be part of the response: alteration in receptor function and side effects occurs, early while the response is delayed.

Adequate length of treatment

Clinicians are only too well aware that the antidepressants currently available unfortunately do not produce a rapid 'cure'. We are accustomed to seeing the optimistic claims of early onset of action made for each new antidepressant as it is introduced being replaced by the more realistic acknowledgement that the treatment of depression remains a slow business. Patients, on the other hand, may be less well-informed about this drawback of antidepressants and come with the expectation of rapid relief. It requires considerable communication skills on the part of the clinician as well as an act of faith on the part of the patient to achieve continued compliance with a treatment which initially seems to have little apparent effect.

Table 14.4. Getting the best out of treatment.

1. Belief in the treatment
2. Prompt treatment
3. Reassurance
4. Information about course of illness, treatment, and side effects
5. Adequate dosage
6. Help compliance
   (a) prefer antidepressants with fewer side effects
   (b) start at low dose and then raise if side effects are likely to be a problem
   (c) where possible use side effects to patient's advantage
7. Adequate length of treatment:
   continue treatment in all cases for 4 months after apparent response

Once past the early stage of treatment, when patients may have felt more in the way of side effects than relief from their depressive illness, compliance with treatment becomes easier as positive effects begin to be felt. For although 4 weeks may be needed for the reliable demonstration of a significant difference between an antidepressant and placebo,[5] substantial improvement in symptomatology can occur, of course, much sooner than this. However, these early signs of response, welcomed by both practitioner and patient, may paradoxically cause some patients to discontinue treatment too soon. A patient who was perhaps initially somewhat reluctant to take medication perceives the improvement in some symptoms as evidence that treatment is no longer required rather than as one stage in the course of recovery. Fortunately the lengthy period of treatment of the acute phase of the illness until the symptoms have resolved will be accepted by most patients if sufficient explanation is provided.

Table 14.4 summarises the main points for getting the best out of antidepressant therapy.

Long-term treatment

Patients are understandably relieved when their symptoms ease and the depression lifts. For many it has been a long gruelling illness and they are only too willing to stop the antidepressant, especially when they have suffered from unpleasant side effects. Two thirds of patients in general practice stop taking the prescribed antidepressant by the end of a month which represents inadequate treatment. This is often a mistake: doctors should stress the need for treatment to continue for fully 4 months in all patients after symptoms have resolved to stabilise and confirm recovery.

It is at this point that patients may express their reluctance to continue treatment because they think the problems of long-term treatment with benzodiazepines occur with antidepressants as well, and they are afraid of dependence on drugs. The advice will need to be repeated that antidepressants as a class are not associated with tolerance or dependence and that they will find it easy to stop taking them. Help in counselling depressed patients to complete the course of treatment with antidepressants will have a remarkable effect in reducing morbidity.

REFERENCES

1. Johnson D.A.W. (1981). Depression: treatment compliance in general practice. *Acta Psychiatrica Scandinavica*, **63** (Suppl. 290), 447–453.
2. Johnson D.A.W. (1973). The treatment of depression in general practice. *British Medical Journal*, **2**, 18–20.

3. Tyrer P. (1978). Drug treatment of psychiatric patients in general practice. *British Medical Journal*, **2**, 1008–1010.
4. Mant A., Duncan-Jones P., Saltman D., Bridges–Webb C., Kehoe L., Lansbury G. and Chancellor A.H.B. (1988). Development of long term use of psychotropic drugs by general practice patients. *British Medical Journal*, **296**, 251–254.
5. Morris J.B. and Beck A.T. (1974). The efficacy of antidepressant drugs. *Archives of General Psychiatry*, **30**, 667–674.

Index